# EL ELYON

## *Fact or Fiction?*

REV. GARY EMAS AND MICKI EMAS

authorHOUSE®

*AuthorHouse™*
*1663 Liberty Drive*
*Bloomington, IN 47403*
*www.authorhouse.com*
*Phone: 1 (800) 839-8640*

*Published by AuthorHouse 10/16/2018*

*ISBN: 978-1-5462-5133-0 (sc)*
*ISBN: 978-1-5462-5131-6 (hc)*
*ISBN: 978-1-5462-5132-3 (e)*

*Library of Congress Control Number: 2018903773*

*Print information available on the last page.*

# CONTENTS

## CHAPTER 1

# THE TRAIN, CONDUCTOR AND SON

### "Zachary Goes to Church"

Today we are not going to write a book that depicts the story of Jesus Christ in this chapter. Many christian writers, pastors, teachers or evangelists when leading people to Jesus Christ as their Lord and Savior they would speak from Matthew, Mark, Luke and John. This is what they have done for thousands of years to lead people to the Lord. We are going to do something different than the norm by introducing a character and his name is Zachary. He was a young man in his early 30's with dark hair and a groomed beard. He was about 5'8" and weighed about 158 lbs. Zachary has been spreading the gospel in a different manner than people are accustomed. The word has gotten out that this new type of evangelist is showing up all over the United States. He must have had an amazing publicist since he is already booked all through the entire year. The only thing that he requires is that they have children and teenagers through the age of 18 to listen to The Train, Conductor and Son. As a car approaches from the south side of town and begins to park, it is Zachary in his BMW with no visible plates on the front. As he reaches over the passenger side seat and pulls out from his brown valise a brown hardback book titled: The Train, Conductor and Son. He exits his car as he looks around to make sure it is safe to leave with the book under his arm and then proceeds to walk across the street. He then notices on the marquee of the church, welcome Zachary Smith to the Pickney Bible Church, Pastor Elias Wallace, Senior Pastor. And with a big smile proceeds to walk into the church. The dialogue would go something like this.

As he approaches a middle-aged man in blue jeans with a gray sweater, the man notices Zachary is wearing a white shirt and a pair of blue jeans. He said to Zachary welcome to the Pickney Bible Church as he extends his hand. Can I call you Zach, Elias says, and you can call me Elias? Zach has a jovial smile on his face and says, yes that will be fine. Where would you like me to set up? Elias has him follow him through a long corridor where the sounds of children and adults are heard. The pastor introduces the congregation to Zachary Smith and lets them know that he is the author of The Train, Conductor and Son. He then says to all the children that they should sit on the floor and the teenagers should sit on the chairs and then we will get this show on the road. Without further ado, I give you Zachary Smith as the crowd begins to applaud. Zachary steps up and lays the book on the pulpit. Before he begins he tells them to bow their heads and says a prayer.

## "Zachary reads from The Train, Conductor and Son"

Dear Lord, thank you for being you. Thank you for allowing me to meet these nice people at this small humble church. I pray that you bless them 30, 60 and 100-fold in this lifetime or the next. I pray those who don't have a relationship with you or understanding about you will finally be cleared up today. I ask that you have every ear attentive and every eye open to the message of The Train, Conductor and Son. In Jesus name we pray, Amen.

He then opens the book and begins to read. The letters miraculously show up on the pages that were written for the first time. He says imagine your families from young to old going on a picnic. Zachary looks out over the people. He bends his knees for comfort, and you decide to take your family on a train ride. While on the train everyone is laughing and telling stories. All of a sudden out of nowhere a thunderstorm appears. As the rain pelts on the window panes, the sound of thunder and flash of lightning are seen in the distance. Meanwhile there is a problem arising miles down the track that is unknown to the conductor. The lightning has struck the bridge and it has plummeted to the river below. This will make it impossible for the train to cross the bridge without also falling into the river. Up ahead the conductor is notified of impending dangers. Unless they switch to another track, they will all fall into a watery grave and they will all die. Zachary says I want you to close your eyes. I want you to imagine yourself on that train very excited, only worrying about the picnic that you are about to go on. You can see yourself playing games with all your family. Now keep your eyes closed, keep imagining being on that train. You don't know what is up ahead because you can't see it.

## "The Conductor Calls the CEO of the Train"

After the conductor gets the news about the mishap he calls and talks to the CEO of the train company. He then asks the advice from the CEO, what should we do? Of course, the CEO of the train snaps to action without hesitation as he begins to speak to the conductor and he begins to say in affirmation, yes sir, yes sir, yes sir. The conductor advises everyone on the train about the impending danger by loudspeaker. They have everything under control and the owner of the train is sending a switchman to switch the track, so they can live.

The son who is the switchman jumps into a pickup truck and barrels toward the switch on track 9. On his way he is met with so many obstacles like heavy wind, rain and lightning. Just before he gets to the switch a nail crashes through the drivers side glass severing his artery in his wrist. Then another nail crashes through the glass on the passenger side and severs the artery on the other wrist. The son in his weakening condition finds his way to the switch box which is called Golgotha. He exits the vehicle and he can hear the sounds and screams of the people as the train as it is reaching the point of no return. He must switch the track now, or they will never be seen again. While he is trying to switch the track, he gets his foot caught in the track on a loose nail that goes through his foot from the top to the bottom. He then must make a decision; do I switch the track back to 9 and they all die, or do I switch it to track 7 where the nail has pierced my foot and they will be saved and I will die for them? The son makes a split-second decision and gives up his life. As the train is approaching track nine to be switched to track 7 the people notice a solitary figure that is hanging on the track and the train kills him. The blood spews all over the people through the window panes. The conductor sees what happened and contacts the owner that his son has died. Then as the conductor heard from the father he said yes your son did give his life to save these people. All the people on the train are remorseful for what they saw. Some even said, one had to die so we could all live. There were even people that said, why would a man die for me? I wouldn't do that. I love my life too much. Another would say, I'm not even worthy enough and look what he did. He then sits down in his seat and cries.

**"Zachary Prepares to Become El Elyon"**

As Zachary begins to slowly close the book, he could heard the sobs of the entire congregation. He then looks at the pastor and he says, now it is your turn pastor. I just set them up. A lot of people asked, how can we get this book to give to others? And the pastor tells the people I have his number and I will call him. As Zachary exits the church he notices that the birds are chirping as the sun beats down on his brow, he transforms himself from Zachary Smith to El Elyon. Back in the building the pastor forgot to thank him, and he had a check for him. He runs frantically to catch him and give him the check. He then looks at the marquee and miraculously the marquee changes to read, for God so loved the world he gave his only begotten son, for who so ever believeth in him should not parish but have everlasting life. John 3:16. As he approaches his car and opens the door he could hear the pastor calling after him. I have your check, I have your check! As he says it the second time with a bewildered look, he realizes Zachary has changed to El Elyon. As the car goes down the street away from the church the pastor notices the license plate. On the black license plate John 3:16 is printed at the top in red letters as is El Elyon in large print in the center of the plate. As the car goes over the horizon he notices something, that the car vanishes. With a puzzled look on his face he remembered what the words El Elyon meant. It meant God of the Hebrews. And he whispers to himself, we were truly blessed today, for Jesus Christ himself was in our midst and we didn't even know.

## "Footnotes"

This book, especially this chapter was designed to help the X factor people (age 12-35), the ones that always say – who, what, when, where and why and not always in that order. I hope the Train, Conductor and Son gave you an outlook on John 3:16. As you begin to peruse these chapters and the evidence begins to mount up – is it **Fact or Fiction**? You make that decision.

# CHAPTER 2

# "THE DEAD SEA SCROLLS REVEALED"

## INTRODUCTION OF THE DEAD SEA SCROLLS

The story has to be told for people to believe in the visitation. We know of the existence of Gods' Angels from what other people have said and done. This writers question is – why are so many people trying to hide the existence of Jesus Christ in his silent years? So many authors from the time parchment could be written upon, have tried to tell the truth. Isn't this what we are trying to do? Here is my question – Why did the Catholic Church, all the way to the Vatican cease to allow the Acropha

Gospel? Over 3000 books were banned from 1940 to 1948 of the existence of Jesus Christs silent years. I believe there are no accidents in the body of Christ. For over 2000 years men, women and children of all races, colors and creeds have been blinded from the truth. Jesus said, and I quote "So if the Son sets you free, you will be free indeed." – John 8:36.

In the 2000 years since his death and resurrection the church has tried to squelch the learning of Jesus Christ as not only the Son of God, but God himself. As quoted by John the Revelator – "And the word became flesh and made his dwelling among us. We have seen his glory, the glory of the one and only Son, who came from the Father, full of. "- John 1:14

## "Swayed by Every Wind of Doctrine"

The Muslim religion believes in the Quran that Jesus Christ was no more than a prophet. The Jews that were responsible for the crucifixion of Jesus Christ, their Messiah, was no more than a Rabbi and a great teacher of the law. The Buddhist believed that Jesus Christ was the Enlightened One. The Catholics show him still on a cross and not showing him risen as the Son of God and treat the Virgin Mary as a Deity God over Him. They spend trillions of dollars on beads, statues and medallions of Virgin Mary. Could these people be swayed by every wind of doctrine that Jesus spoke about? The Baptist adhere to their teachings, but how do they become Baptists since the religion came about in the early 1800's. John the Baptizer is how they base it. They believe that when the Apostles all died off, so did the gifts of God. The Quakers of the 1600's were more apt to follow the teachings of Jesus Christ. After all they left a tyranny and persecution of king monarchs.

### "Who's Telling the Truth"

So, let's recap this chapter. We know if we go to the Tomb of Mohammed, he is still there. If you go to the Tomb of Buddha you will find he is still there, bones and all. If you go to the Tomb of Mary, she is still there. So that removes all doubt that she is a Deity of God or a miracle worker. But if you go to the Tomb of Jesus Christ (by the way, it was a borrowed tomb) He is risen. In order to know the truth from fiction, I think we have scientifically drawn a case for Jesus Christ.

### "Dead Sea Scrolls Uncovered in Less than 2000 Years and Why"

Remember I told you this author is trying to tell a story. Is this fiction of non-fiction? Why did God wait almost 2000 years to unravel the mystery of the Bible? So, in 1947 a Palestinian boy was tending his flock of goats around the Dead Sea and the Dead Sea Caves. As the arid winds were cutting through his olive skin, he was like any other young man with curly dark hair, olive skin, adorned with goat skin apparel and moccasins. It was a bright day as the sun shone down on the boy. The name of the Bedouin boy is unimportant to the story. But what he does next will change history from fiction to fact. As he tends his sheep, the bells are heard from their collars and the chatter from his friend as he exclaims to his friend, have you seen my baby goat (with a concerned look)? His friend says I think he is in a cave ahead of us. They head to one of the caves. The boy reached down and picked up a pebble and threw it into the cave. We heard a thud and then the sound as something breaks, and the boys run into to cave. At their surprise they unraveled the Mystery of The Dead Sea Scrolls, which had been hidden for over 2000 years. They were kept in vessels made of clay and the scrolls were stored inside to protect them from the elements. When this cave is set to excavate the excavators find well over 1000 scrolls of parchment and fragments in 11 caves. They would carbon date these items from 408 BC to 323 AD.

Back in biblical times from the time of minor prophets to major prophets, they would always use scribes. The teacher would give the words to place on the parchment, sometimes made of papyrus while others were animal skins, that would later be written and told by the scribe. Were they the keeper of the word for God? This story teller believes that to be true.

According to historians there was an order called the Essenes. They were a sect of Second Temple Judaism that flourished from the 2nd century BC to the 1st century AD. Some scholars claim they seceded from the Zodacite priests. Some people believe that this ended the reign of these temple protectorants of the Dead Sea Scrolls. I believe that these people were not only the protectorant of the Dead Sea Scrolls that were told by God they also knew by the sun, moon and stars that the Rise of the Last High Priest was coming. As they too saw the Jupiter and Bethlehem stars along with the comet approaching.

Before the Roman Empire invaded the land of Israel this lonely sect of religious people would flee for their lives and head to a place called Qumran in the Judean desert. So, this means that the Essene order still exists to modern day time and they were the true keeper of the Dead Sea Scrolls.

Now remember I told you earlier there is a reason why God picked these two witnesses for him. One of the Bedouin boys who found the Dead Sea Scrolls decided to take one of the fragments. He then placed it in his brown leather pouch as he was leaving with the goats. Yeah that's right he found the goat. They headed toward their camp and placed it on the post overnight. The Bedouin boy – early in the morning was met by a shoe cobbler. While discussing what he found he shows the cobbler the fragment. And the dialogue would go something like this: The cobbler said, this leather will make a fine pair of sandals. I have a customer who is an archeologist who would have the sandals I will make for him. The Bedouin boy says I need $4.00 and it is yours. The cobbler reaches into his belt and pulls out a money pouch and counts out $4.00 and hands it to the boy. The boy hands the piece of animal skin to the cobbler. Then the cobbler goes to his shop and begins to work on making the sandals for the architect. Did God in his intimate wisdom foreshadow that the Bedouin boy would give the cobbler an animal skin for only $4.00 mind you, and how many chances in a million would there be that a cobbler would buy a piece of skin and make a pair of sandals and sell them to an archeologist? He would then in turn see the inscriptions on the bottom of the sandals scribed in Aramaic, Hebrew and Greek. These words were works of the Old Testament. This archeologist was responsible for the excavation of the Dead Sea Caves and finding 1500 fragments of the Dead Sea Scrolls. The scrolls were made of papyrus and animal skins. Like I told you earlier, God is not the author of confusion, God is the finisher of our faith. To prove that this is a legitimate occurrence three days later, after the dig was over there was an advertisement placed in the New York Times. The advertisement would read, "Four fragments of the Dead Sea Scrolls are for sale for $250,000.00. That afternoon the founder of those fragments was given a cashiers check in the amount that he requested.

## "The Clock is Ticking, and Time is Running Out"

When the archeologists from 1947 to 1956 had excavated the 11 caves in the Judean desert, they had remarked how could these have been saved for 2000 years. The answer was obvious. The sect of religious keepers put them in such a way to preserve them by wrapping them in a linen cloth, that they also used to wrap a mummy. Then they placed them in a vessel. They were trying to tell the world of the existence of Jesus Christ, that he would be laid in a borrowed tomb and have linen cloth wrapped around his body. They wanted to let people believe that Jesus Christ was The Last High Priest. Yet the time was running out as these archeologists, scientists and other workers were constantly touching the scrolls as delicately as they possibly could because they were so fragile they were breaking apart. They devised various ways in the University in Israel to maintain their longevity as well preserve them. But still, time was running out. How long could these scrolls withstand all the examinations? Then after 40 years a man from the United States, Dr. Zuckerman came up with a program that would last forever. They digitized the Dead Sea Scrolls.

## "Footnotes"

In this chapter we are showing more evidence to support this theory that God used a Gentile instead of a Jew or a Christian. The Dead Sea Scrolls gave us the answer that many of the religious sect have tried to hide. We introduce the Essene Order as the protectorant. Then 2000 years later we show a Bedouin boy of Muslim faith, by accident found these ancient writings. With the assistance of the cobbler and then the archeologist, discovered one of the most important archeological digs of the 20<sup>th</sup> century. Why were the silent years of Jesus Christ banned by the Vatican from 1940 – 1948? Was Heaven crying out to find the truth? Fact or Fiction? "It is in your court now".

# CHAPTER 3

# "THE RISE OF THE IMMORTAL PRIEST OF SALEM OF MELCHIZEDEK BY THE ORDER OF EL ELYON"

## (THE MOST HIGH GOD)

And Melchizedek – king of Salem brought forth bread and wine: and he was the priest of the most high God. And he blessed him, and said, blessed be Abram of the most high God, possessor of heaven and earth. And blessed be the most high God, which hath delivered thine enemies into thy hand. And he gave him tithes of all. Genesis 14:18-20.

He brought wine and bread and broke bread with Abram and King of Sodom. Psalms 76:2

## "The Seed Has Now Been Planted"

The scholars have said with the examination of the Dead Sea Scrolls, that they were about to see the shift from Mt. Sinai which is under Moses law that was given by God the 10 Commandments in the desert region of Mt. Sinai to Mt. Calvary. And this is where Jesus Christ would plant the seed of Christianity to the world. There are so many religions today that would have done anything to stop this wave. Even today Christianity flourishes.

He said, "I am the voice of the one crying out in the wilderness, Make straight the way of the Lord; as the prophet Isaiah said" John 1:23

## "One will water the Seed"

I planted the seed and Apollos watered it, but God made it grow. So, neither he who plants nor he who waters is anything, but only God, who makes things grow. 1 Corinthians 3:6-7. The story teller is about to tell the story about why these things are happening. It's like God is trying to make amends for everything that has happened in the past, present and leading up to the future. I have heard people in todays society as well as long past, call God a coward. After all, God knows everything, he sees everything, and he hears everything. You hear of mothers saying why did my child have to die, why did my child have to get sick and why now? What did they do to you? The calamity and destruction of mankind in this world has brought on such an atrocity because of their free will. There is good and evil in this world. It does exist, and I have seen it, but the devil and his co-horts do not care about free will. I have listened to so many people blame God for everything, from wars to pestilence to earthquakes and other national disasters. When a fire breaks out, is God trying to purge sin out of the world or when a tornado ravages a land like a knife cutting butter, is that purging the land?

## "The Set Up"

So, what is God thinking? Why doesn't he take everyone who knows Him up to Heaven and send the others that are evil to Hell? But I don't believe that is how God saw this world set up. I believe when sin entered this world, not when Lucifer fell to the second heaven, but when Adam and Eve sinned, that is when the decision in Heaven had to be made.

# CHAPTER 4

# THE FIRST SUPPER

## "The King Prepares for Earth"

In heaven the Godheads had all come together and unanimously decided that Jesus would be the one to enter this sinful world. They lined up all the angels according to their ranks and titles and they all sat down for the first supper. Jesus was at the head of the table and said, I must leave you for a little while. There was a hush as everyone was drinking from the water goblets and then they stopped at his remark. Then his chief general who had 9 sets of wings and stood 9 feet tall said to El Elyon. "There must be another way my Lord". There was a remark heard from the cloud.

"SILENCE". It was as if a pin dropped and Father God came out of the cloud, adorned in a white robe, golden sandals and white woven beard and walks to the head of the table to El Elyon. He states that El Elyon must die for all the sins of the world, past, present and future, so all humanity can live. And the dialogue would go something like this: As the 9 foot angel with the 9 sets of wings said – in a deep voice, Lord what would El Elyon be called on Earth? He walks over to the angels Gabriel and Raphael – the fiery seraphim and tells Gabriel of the 21st of September, according to the earthly calendar in the year 3 BC you will go and perform the 3rd duty I have instructed you to do over the last 6 months. That day is approaching, Raphael, as he puts his hands on his shoulder and says, and you will prepare to be the bright light when He is born into the world. Then he looks at all the others at the table and says many of you will be needed for battle when my son is born. As they bow their heads, for Lucifer will try to do everything he can to stop him from being born as they stare at each other in disgust. Then his father retreats into the cloud. El Elyon remarks, we have been planning this ever since we shut out Adam and Eve from the garden of Eden. I will be called upon at one point to be the last high priest. I will take my blood and sprinkle it in the real holies of holy in Mt. Zion. Now let us feast, El Elyon said and drink. And they did. I must go away for a couple of days and set up my arrival by the sun, the moon and the stars. Gabriel, El Elyon says, when you see the sun, moon and stars begin to align, you will also see two other things occur that my father and I have talked about. When the moon is at full twilight on the 21st of September 3 BC you will see my star, the planet Jupiter align with the moon. There will be an alignment of 9 planets and Regulus retrograding of the virgin. Then Jesus says to another angel, you will be responsible for the Bethlehem star and you must make sure that exactly midnight on the first day of the new moon that it will be over the City of David, Bethlehem. The star will begin on that date and will end exactly two years later. There is a reason for that and he turns and smiles. As he raises his drink to his lips and says to the angel on his right, you will be the keeper of the comet for over 3000 years and it will be called Lovejoy. You must prepare tonight to put everything in motion my friends. Remember Lucifer will try to do everything like my father said, so we have to make sure everything goes off without a hitch.

## "No One Knows the Date, the Time or the Hour"

The definition of no one knows the date, the time or the hour is not what Christians, pastors or teachers have given as the representation of the rapture. As a matter of fact there is no representation of the rapture in the Bible. In the year 1830, a man by the name of Wycliff created the Scofield Bible to show the existence of the so called rapture. For about 300 years the Christian world is trying to get a free pass to heaven without consequences. God is looking for a church of love without spot or blemish

If we have learned anything from the mistakes of the Acts Church, Jesus told them to tarry in Jerusalem for 50 days. The purpose of this obedience was to get the apostles to be with one mind and one accord. Their dialogue would go something like this: The voices were heard of not only the apostles but of the elect also. As the voices become unruly, the ruler of the sect named Peter said "stop". Would our Lord like us to be fighting amongst ourselves? Thomas the doubter said, what gave you the right Peter to be the spokesman for us all? As they all begin to murmur again and Jesus mother stepped in front of Thomas and put her hand on his heart and said – with a soft voice – is this why my son died? She then walks around in a circle and places her hand on each one of their hearts one by one. She then sits down in the chair and all the apostles sit next to her. She says, I want to tell you a story no one knows about. My son explained to me after Joseph died that you (I) were just a vessel being used by my Father in Heaven. He then took me outside and showed me the kiln where we made our pottery. If you broke this kiln, how would you be able to make another piece of pottery? Then Mary said I guess you would have to use someone elses kiln.

Now you understand mother why God used a borrowed kiln. What you don't know is that I have 7 boys and three beautiful girls for allowing God to use my vessel – my kiln.

Jesus told me that one day people would try to praise me and lift me to a diety state. You see children, there is only one God and his name is El Elyon. Here on earth he is known as my son – Jesus Christ, the only begotten son of God. It is time Peter and my son John and you Thomas to put aside your differences, all of you. If it takes us to fast and pray, that's what we are going to do.

When El Elyon was speaking about these occurrences, it was done. on a parchment or papyrus and a scribe wrote down the words in the following languages – Hebrew, Greek and Aramaic. So, when you are looking at the truth like this storyteller has been reiterating over and over, is it fact or fiction? If we were to fact check this, we would come to a very important conclusion. "That is that no one knows the date, the time or the hour and I will reiterate this over and over and I will rehash it with you over and over again. That is not the rapture. The definition means that when the two witnesses, and those are the ones that were commissioned by the King and at that time it was Herod the Tetrac, a descendent of the Edomites. They would look for the alignment of the stars and the new moon. When the new moon was discovered they would go back to the King with this knowledge and the King would call for the keepers of the shofar to sound the 100 blasts and the festival trumpets have just begun ushering in the new year.

## "Footnotes"

In Chapter 4 we again try to link together this myth that no one knows the date, the time or the hour. We again as storytellers have explained in detail what is the definition, what mistakes the Acts Church made and the two sacred animals of God and how it would all end at the Labyrinth of the road that leads to Jerusalem. Fact or fiction? Pray about it and see what God shows you. You may be amazed.

CHAPTER 5

# THE REAL BIRTH OF CHRIST

The sign of Christ being born was not only seen by the three Magi, the shepherds keeping their flocks in the Bethlehem hills and the sages and magicians of the King who were the keeper of astrology, but by God himself and the angels. The Audience of one who has the best seat in the house.

## "September 21, 3 BC"

A very select group of people want you to believe that Jesus was born on December 25, 1 AD. We have seen many stories, movies, children's books relating to this date. Even though this is a brisk wintery time of year in Bethlehem they amass a fortune with their Nativity Scenes, baby Jesus and their replicas of times long gone. The crowds would be hustling back and forth as they prepared for their religious festivities. The only problem with that statement is when God was talking about the seasons, he wasn't saying about the winter, spring, summer or fall he was talking about the 7 seasons that the Jews followed on their calendar. So, let's look at this for a second and try to interpret what would be the busiest time of the season for Jesus to be born. Some people, even scholars of today or evangelists have made assumptions that he was born on the day he died – Passover. Yet, if that was true then why was it winter months that start in the beginning of September and end the end of December? Herdsmen and shepherds would have left their animals in caves to prevent them from dying from exposure and theft. So, the busiest time of the year would have been, of course Rosh Hashanah which is the new year leading up to Yom Kippur. There would be no doubt in my mind that this would be the date with the alignment of the constellations of the 9 planets and the 3 stars. This is found in the book of Revelation 12:2.

## "The Three Magi"

Gasper, Balthasar and Melchior

They were decendents of Seth, the third son of Adam. They were from the settlement known as Seir, which is a land in China.

They were from Babylon. Daniel 5. They were astrologists, part of the Zooralism. As they saw the unusual star in the sky and they followed it to the outskirts of the City of David known as Bethlehem. For they felt in their spirit that Herod was deceptive so all three of them went to Herod and asked him where they can find the King? This is how the dialogue would go: He said I am the King. Have you come to worship me, as he sits back proudly on his throne with a crown and a golden scepter in his hand? As the spokesman for the three Magi's – named Balthazar, Balthazar points to the heavens and says to the pompous King, we have followed the star – the planet Jupiter and we are looking for the child who will one day be called the King of Kings and Lord of Lords. Then Herod says with a disdained laugh and bellows to the Magi's, when you find him, tell me where he can be found, and I will worship him as well. They bowed to the King in reverence and continued their journey. Then Gasper, the smallest of the three Magi's, said God has given me a revelation and we are to follow the star and not come back the same way we came for fear of our lives. So, as they journeyed with their caravans outside the City of David and began to move to where the star was headed, but not the City of David. God told Gasper to head to the borders of Egypt and wait.

## "They All Moved to the City of David"

Of course, the story always tells us the Christ Child is about to be born. The shepherd was tending his father's flock along with his friend. When suddenly, out of the East, on the cold but clear night was a comet that flew across the sky and frightened the shepherd and his friend. And the dialogue would go like this: What was that exclaimed the shepherd boy as they cowered in fear? And his friend said, I don't know. Then another star appeared over the City of David, and looked as if it had stopped. But something was different about this star because it seemed to illuminate the sky around Bethlehem. And then an angel appeared blowing a golden shofar. When he had blown the 100 blast of blessings he lowered it and placed it on his belt. He shone like an ultra-bright light so that they had to cover their eyes. Then he uttered, I am the Angel Gabriel to bring a message from God, to fear not. For in the City of David, born tonight as the planets align is a Baby Child and his name is Immanuel. That means God is with him. He will be called wonderful. As the light dimmed and he lowered his body to earth and stood before them, and they beheld him as he went to each one and laid his hand on their heads as he kneeled before them. He then grabbed their arms and told them to rise. He said, I am not worthy with a soft subtle voice, that you should kneel before me, as he puts his arms around the waist of the shepherd. I am just a servant and messenger of the Most High known as El Elyon. And then he said he will be called Counselor, Everlasting Father, and Prince of Peace. Go to him in the City of David. He will be a baby wrapped in swaddling clothes and lying in a manger. And his name will be Jesus. They are now in the back of the inn which is a cave. Go and be a witness to the birth of your Messiah and follow the star. Then he rose and was gone. So, the shepherd along with his friend and the flock begin their journey over the Judean desert hills. They were following the instructions from the Angel Gabriel.

## "Mary and Joseph Arrive at the Inn"

Meanwhile, on this brisk wintery night 2 lonely figures enter into Bethlehem. The man, wearing a cloak which covered him from head to toe was leading a donkey to a place of comfort.

He sees an inn off in a far distance. And the dialogue would go something like this: Joseph, Mary said with a weakening voice, I feel that Jesus is about to be born. Please hurry. Mary, Joseph said, El Elyon is with us. He will guide us and lead us, as he points to a star over Bethlehem. The woman known as Mary was also keeping herself warm by the garments she wore, Mary said to Joseph, hurry my beloved. I am weak from this journey and I am hungry. Joseph said, Mary we are almost there. Have faith he says as she nods in reverence. Joseph said to Mary as they were forcing their way through a crowd, here is an inn, let's see if we can find a room and she agreed. As he gently lifted her off the donkey and they entered through the wooden doors of the inn, they were approached immediately by a tall scruffy looking man. He said to Joseph and Mary "STOP", we are filled up. For as you see it is the time of our new year called Rosh Hashanah. But sir, Joseph said, my wife is about to give birth as he looked upon her with reverence and smiled. The man said, there is a cave, it is not much but we keep our animals there to keep them from the blistering cold. If you go there, my servant will help you with anything that you need. I will have my wife help you with anything you need as she is the midwife of Bethlehem and has delivered many babies. My servant will bring you and your wife food, water and wine for the celebration of the blessed event. Also, my servant will take your donkey and give him hay and water and bed him down for the night. As Mary smiles in acknowledgement of his generous offer and Joseph said to the innkeeper, thank you. The servant boy leads them all to the cave, including the donkey. Joseph says to Mary in a soft voice as he clutches her tightly. Mary, look. He points to the the cave entrance door. In Hebrew – is an inscription that says - El Elyon and the boy marvels. He says to Joseph and Mary – sir, what does that mean? Joseph says it means God of the Hebrews. Again he says – God of the Hebrews. He unlocks the door to the cave and they all enter. Joseph with the aid of the servant lay Mary down on a bed of straw to comfort her for which might be a long ordeal. Then as a middle aged, short stocky woman with a hooded cloak enters into the cave she says, my name is Rachel. I am the wife of Eli the innkeeper. Where is the woman who is going to give birth? Joseph politely says this is my wife Mary who is the one about to give birth. Then she claps her hands together and says, Samuel start bedding down their donkey. Then Joseph reacting to her command saw an eating trough and removed all the straw. Then the woman looks at Mary and says, my dear, don't be afraid for I have delivered thousands of children in Bethlehem. Mary smiles and says to Rachel, thank you. May God richly bless you and your husband for this random act of kindness. May God bless you amongst all women. Unaware to them all, a fiery angel lightens the sky to Heaven. As the boy falls, the angel lifts him up and says to him, fear not, for tonight in the City of David will be born your Messiah. His name will be Jesus Christ, the Son of God. And the moment that happened the Angels in heaven began to sing;

Holy, Holy, Holy

Lord God Almighty

The Heaven is full with his Glory

Peace on Earth Good Will to Men

The angel turns to Mary and Joseph and says my name is Raphael. I am a fiery cherub. I am here to be a witness for heaven, of the birth of our king. You have met already in many times and many places the angel Gabriel. They both nodded.

He said to all that was there including the animals, it is time. For it has been ordained that he would be born at the appointed time. Behold the Lamb of God that will taketh away the sins of the world. As he reaches his finger to heaven, fire shoots out of it and the door swings open. A sweet cry begins to come forth between the legs of Mary. Raphael then takes a golden blanket that is wrapped around his belt and miraculously delivers Jesus and places him in a feeding trough filled with straw. As this miracle from God occurs, the shepherd boy and his friend along with the sheep have found the star and have come to be the witness of the birth of Jesus. The heavenly host now starts to sing:

**"Handel's Messiah"**

Hallelujah, Hallelujah

Hallelujah, Hallelujah Hallelujah [3x]

For the Lord God omnipotent reigneth

Hallelujah, Hallelujah, Hallelujah, Hallelujah [2x]

For the Lord God omnipotent reigneth [3x]

Hallelujah

The kingdom of this world

Is become

The kingdom of our God

And of His Christ

And He shall reign forever

King of Kings

For ever and ever

And Lord of Lords

Then Gabriel appears shining bright above the cave. Then people from the inn as well as the town begin to witness the blessing.

Gabriel pulls out his shofar, looks up to heaven and proudly blows the blessing on the new child. Meanwhile at a far off distance, the 3 Magi have pulled over and are in restful slumber. They are awakened from the fire shooting up to heaven and the sound of the Shofar. They all hug together in happiness. As Gasper says to the other 2 kings, remember we are not to go there until God tells us to go there. Then Gabriel and the fiery cherub Raphael tell the people that this is truly the Messiah. The government will be upon his shoulders for he will be one day be your sacrificial lamb that you raise in the City of David, Bethlehem. Remember these words, keep them in your heart and know that Jesus, known as El Elyon is with you. Aslo that he will rise to be your Last High Priest. The angels disappear into the night.

### "Jesus is Now Two Years Old"

After Jesus was born, according to his Jewish custom he would be circumcised by a Levite priest who would perform the brisk. Then after 40 days Joseph would be required to register him as a new birth. Forty has always been a trial number with God. It is called a time of testing and trials. A time of purity, fasting, praying that is required by God for your obedience. So many people, even in todays society believe in the 40. Times of testings, and trials, praying and fasting. But the problem with today is they don't practice what they preach. They are all wanting to worship him in spirit and truth but they forgot their first love. It seems like everybody tries to find the answer, but it's not with God and I don't understand why. On June 6, 1944 the President of the United States later in the afternoon was in the white house surrounded by microphones and was ready to give a speech that we had invaded Europe. But what they got was a prayer. A prayer that would lead us and guide us. A prayer of fasting and praying to ask God to not only protect our boys but every man, woman and child of the USA. So as a Christian man who loved the Lord adhered to this 40 day rule.

So Jesus, Mary and Joseph were not only protected by God for the tyranny that was about to befall them from King Herod from being annihilated. An angel Gabriel came to Joseph and Mary at night and said with a soft voice, Mary – Joseph it is time for you to leave. The king is looking to seek you out. For his soldiers have told him as the new year approaches, of Jesus who is now reaching the age of two and that the 3 wise men from the East, when they left went the opposite way. So now they are going to be looking for you. Take nothing with you as this way they will believe that you are still here. For provision will be provided by your Father. The angels will guard your steps so do not be afraid. As friends knock on the door, and the conversation would go something like this: Joseph says hello my friends. What are you doing here? As Gabriel says, these are your guides that will take you to the outskirts or borders of Egypt where you will meet three men on the last road before Egypt. So move quickly because Herod had decreed every child under the age of two will be slain by his butchers. So Mary, Joseph, Jesus and their guides set out to head for Egypt. No sooner did they get beyond the Judean desert and they heard cries like they had never heard before.

## "Gabriel Appears on the Road to Egypt"

Gabriel says softly – the cries you hear are the mothers and fathers who have lost their children. The king has slain all children from birth to the age of two. As Mary has Jesus on her shoulders, he turns as to look towards Bethlehem and looks up to the stars, raises his hands and lowers his head to pray. As through his spiritual eyes he could see so many of his angels filling up the sky on their way to earth to gather the children to take their spirits to Heaven. And then he turns and whispers into his mothers ear and she smiles and everyone whispers into the next persons ear until all know what has just happened. As angel Gabriel bows down before the King Jesus, the mother of Jesus sets his tiny feet on the ground and he approaches Gabriel and places his little fingers on his head. And a bright countenance shines about him. Then as Jesus turns his little head and looks back at everyone, they all prostrate themselves before Him. Jesus turns back to Gabriel and says to him – well done my good and faithful servant. Then Gabriel stands and says to all present, you will be going down the road for the next 10 days and the angels will always be around you to protect you so don't be afraid of what you might see or hear. You probably won't see me for a while. The next angel you will come in contact with you have never seen before. He is the angel of angels and his name is Michael, our general. Then Gabriel disappears.

## "10 Days Later"

As the group with Jesus is approaching the borders of Egypt and they are following the Bethlehem star, they are met by Michael the archangel. Michael has his sword out of its scabbard and the sword is facing down towards the ground. Then Michael says to Jesus, My Lord, the ground had been hallowed for you to your destination. For we have fought a battle with Lucifer and his fallen angels and have conquered this land. Then he bows down to Jesus. With Jesus being carried by Joseph, Jesus says thank you Michael. This is my mother Mary and Michael stands up and shakes Marys hand and puts his sword back in the scabbard. This is my father Joseph and his friends and Michael shakes Josephs hand. As they are speaking, a caravan appears on the horizon. They can see three silhouetted figures on camels ahead of the caravan.

## "The Three Wisemen Meet Jesus"

As Joseph, Mary and the group begin to put up their camp for the night, the Bethlehem star has now reached above the tent. As Joseph was putting in the last tent peg and making sure that the tent was safe to occupy he saw the three wisemen with crowns on their heads. As they dismounted from their camels Gasper said, I see we are in the right place. Michael the archangel said to them, yes He is here the King of Kings and the Lord of Lords. They reached into their saddlebags and each pulled out a special gift for Jesus.

As Jesus was coming out of the tent with his mother Mary, one gave him gold and laid it at his feet and bowed down. The second one gave him frankincense and laid it at his feet and bowed down. The third wiseman gave him myrrh and laid it at his feet and also bowed down. Then baby Jesus walked over to the wisemen and began to pray over them. As he reached the third one, Jesus said RISE, for I have not come to be king over you but to witness the truth and to be a servant for all mankind. Then he ran over to Mary and held her hand. The tallest of the three wisemen was Balthazar and said, these are just tokens and then he turns his head towards the caravan and waves his right arm and says this is all for you. For when a king is paid homage by us, we want to show how much we honor him. Michael said to Belthazar, I am the archangel Michael. Would you and your caravan like to sup with us and Balthasar said to Michael, yes we would like to join you. He motioned to the servants to begin setting up the tents. Then Michael said to them, when dawn breaks, we will enter into Egypt and you will follow us. When we have reached our destination then you will unload everything. The next morning you and your caravan will depart. God said to Michael to give the wisemen – who were decendents of Seth – a message from him. I have followed you since the third born of Adam. Tomorrow when you head back to your lands you will tell them, all of their wisemen, their sages and soothsayers and Kings that the seed was first planted and now it has to be watered. And their Messiah has been born. And let it be known that this is my Son and the only begotten of the Father of whom I am well pleased. And Jesus looked up to heaven and the star diminished in the sky. After the prophecy of Isaiah has come to pass, God will get the increase.

## "Footnotes"

So is it fact or fiction that Jesus was actually born on Sept. 21, 3BC at the same time the new year began? Is it possible that

Jesus was born on Dec. 25th? I believe the writer would say no. Since everything revolved around the Jewish holidays or the seasons. Since the only 2 that are very important in Jewish history are the Feast of Festivals which as we well know is the Passover and the last is the Feast of Purpose, which is the New Year. What would give God more of an opportunity to introduce the Messiah than those times? Some historians have already signified that St. Nicholas came on Dec. 25th and started in Germany. How long ago was that? Only God knows. But isn't it strange that he had a red suit trimmed in white? Isn't it strange that his world is a world of believers? And where he lives and exists is invisible and you can't see it. In the Bible it says – "God made this world first for the unseen before the seen." Hebrews 11:13 Jesus said in Matthew, you believe because you have seen me. But there are people coming after you that believe but have not seen. Chew on that!

**"Footnote 2"**

So Jesus went to live in Egypt and was taken care of by his Father in Heaven according to Michael the archangel. Jesus grew in stature as a young child until Herods' death. Jesus and his family returned back to Bethlehem but resided in Nazareth. At the same time Mary, mother of Jesus and Joseph, father of Jesus started having their own children because God provided. Probably Joseph taught Jesus to be a carpenter and probably they made furniture for the towns people or the government. I'm pretty sure that they knew what it was like to make crosses. By the time he reached the age of 12 he had known the Torah fluently and could even debate with members of the Sanhedrin. One day after the Passover Jesus was not found for a couple of days. So Mary and Joseph went back with James to Jerusalem and saw him teaching in the temple. Then Joseph said, where have you been my son? Then Jesus looked at his father and said, Don't you know that I would be about my fathers' business? That same year Joseph died at the same time Jesus became a man. (The silent years have now begun.)

# CHAPTER 6

# JEWISH CARPENTER

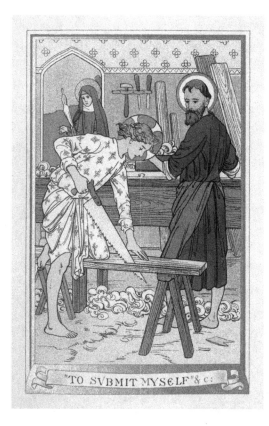

The silent years of Christ are probably the most baffling of all of His life that we learned scholars have tried to understand. Some say that Jesus from the age of twelve, which is the age of accountability for a Jewish boy, took over the care of his family. In the book of Matthew, Joseph is mentioned one last time when Jesus was the age of twelve. He might have died and went to be with the Lord at that time and turned over his business to Jesus as the eldest son's rights and privileges and blessings. Could he have made the furniture and crosses since those were what Jesus saw growing up as a child? Was Jesus accountable to His mother Mary and later His 7 brothers and 3 sisters because of the death of Joseph? Is the age of thirty the age of rabbi or teacher? Who taught him? Was it God? Jesus always said that he testified of His Father, and He knows Him, and His father knows him too.

**"The Hidden Book Revealed"**

With the exception of the miraculous events connected with the birth of Jesus, we know little of the first thirty years of His life upon this earth. When He was eight days old, He was circumcised according to Jewish law (Luke 2:21). Fourty days later he was presented in the temple (Luke 2:22-39). There is the account of the visit of those wise men from the east (Matthew 2:1–12) and then the flight into Egypt to escape the wrath of Herod (Matthew 2:13–23). There is a general reference to His eventual settlement at Nazareth (Matthew 2:23 and Luke 2:39–40) and then the record of a visit to Jerusalem when Jesus was twelve years old (Luke 2:41–50). Following this, there is a blank space in the narrative that covers eighteen years in the life of Christ. Other than the generic notation that He was advancing in wisdom, stature, and in favor with God and men (Luke 2:51–52), we know absolutely nothing of this time span. Are we not curious? Would not an average human biographer have given some interesting data? That is a normal expectation. It was this very circumstance that called forth a number of ancient spurious writings, known collectively as the Apocryphal Gospels. These extracanonical documents arose because of the desire to have a fuller knowledge of certain periods of the life of Christ that the genuine Gospels omitted. Consider, for instance, the Childhood Gospel of Thomas. It depicts the boy Jesus making little birds out of clay and causing them to fly away.

## "Luke The Physician"

The physician is Dr. Luke, called by Paul "the beloved physician" (Colossians 4:14)—a wonderful title for this man. Luke, a medical doctor, used more medical terms in his scriptural record than did Hippocrates, the founder of medicine, in his written records. Dr. Luke is the obstetrician who recorded the birth of Christ. His is the longest record of the virgin birth and properly so. I am not impressed when a so-called theologian in a famous seminary in New York City says that the virgin birth is a biological impossibility. Such a statement reveals his ignorance of biology and his ignorance of impossibilities. Dr. Luke, a medical doctor of the first century, gives us a most comprehensive account.

Not only is he the obstetrician, Dr. Luke is the pediatrician, for he gives us the only account of the boy Jesus. Again, this is properly so.

After the birth of the Lord Jesus Christ, the shepherds went back to their flocks on the hillside. The wise men disappeared into the mysterious east. The angels returned to heaven and shut the door for almost thirty years. And Joseph took the young child with His mother down into Egypt. How long did they stay there? I do not know. We only know that Matthew tells us that they did return:

But when Herod was dead, behold, an angel of the Lord appeareth in a dream to Joseph in Egypt, saying, Arise, and take the young child and his mother, and go into the land of Israel; for they are dead who sought the young child's life. And he arose, and took the young child and his mother, and came into the land of Israel. But when he heard that Archelaus did reign in Judea in the place of his father, Herod, he was afraid to go there; notwithstanding, being warned of God in a dream, he turned aside into the parts of Galilee; and he came and dwelt in a city called Nazareth; that it might be fulfilled which was spoken by the prophets, He shall be called a Nazarene (Matthew 2:19–23).

Matthew gives us the information that when they came out of Egypt, they went up to Nazareth, at which point he drops the record until Christ began His public ministry at thirty years of age. The other Gospel writers do the same thing—with the exception of Dr. Luke.

## "Train Up Your Child so when They get Old, They Won't Depart from It"

From the moment they come out of the land of Egypt, Dr. Luke takes the case. He is the pediatrician. First, let us look at the period of childhood—from birth to adolescence. Dr. Luke lets us look first at his medical chart where the first twelve years are covered by this statement: "And the child grew, and became strong in spirit, filled with wisdom; and the grace of God was upon him" (Luke 2:40). Then from twelve years of age through His teens, here is the statement that is made: "And Jesus increased in wisdom and stature, and in favor with God and man" (Luke 2:52).

The word for "grew" in verse 40 is not the same word as "increased" in verse 52.

"Grew" is a word that Dr. Luke uses very carefully. It is a doctor's word that indicates physical growth. "The child grew, and became strong in spirit" is growth without any sense of responsibility except obedience to authority.

One cause of what is known as juvenile delinquency in our day can be traced back to the parental attitude in the home before the child is twelve years of age. A mother of a six-year-old said to me, "I always call my Willie in and explain to him the reason for everything." What explanation does a six-year-old need? He is to be taught obedience to authority. When he learns obedience to authority until he is twelve years of age, he will not have trouble in his teens. This is child psychology according to God's book— not very popular but mighty good. During those first twelve years, Jesus just grew. Everything was not explained to Him. His mother said, "You are to run on this errand." She did not have to sit down and give Him a lecture on why He should run the errand. The "why" was that He was to obey His parents. Learning obedience in the home ensures obedience to God and other authority when a young person leaves his home. A mother was reading a Bible story to her little boy. It was a story about Jesus. At the conclusion, she did what a mother invariably will do. She said, "Now why can't you be good like the little boy Jesus?" The six-year-old had the answer. He said, "Because He's God, and I'm just your boy." Though Jesus was God, He grew those first twelve years as any child should grow—without responsibility except obedience to authority.

### "Jesus Young Ministry Begins"

When Jesus was at the age of twelve, Dr. Luke thought it was proper to tell us one occurrence in His life that marks a change from childhood to adolescence. It is an isolated incident, and we do not want to miss it, for it is given to bridge the gap from His birth to the time He began His public ministry. The law said that three times a year, the males were to go to Jerusalem. The incident given to us by Dr. Luke was during the Passover feast when Jesus was twelve. They traveled to Jerusalem, as was their custom, together with a great company. It was an informal sort of going, and I do not think there was anything out of the ordinary in the fact that on the return trip, they did not miss Jesus until they had gone a day's journey. But suddenly, they did miss Him. You can imagine the thoughts that must have passed through the mind of Mary. They traced their way back to Jerusalem and found Him in a most unusual place—in the temple, with the doctors of the law, the scribes, and the Pharisees around Him, marveling at the questions He could ask and the answers He could give. But all this was not impressive to Mary. She barged right in, as a mother would. "And when they saw him, they were astonished; and his mother said unto him, Son, why hast thou thus dealt with us? Behold, thy father and I have sought thee, sorrowing" (Luke 2:48).

"Son" is not the word used for "child" in verse 40 nor is it the word used in verse 52. It is a term of endearment—her mother word for Him. She called Him Son in a way that no one else could have called Him. "Son, why hast thou thus dealt with us?" Now note this: "Behold, thy father and I have sought thee, sorrowing." Father? Yes. By virtue of the fact that he was the husband of Mary, he was Jesus's father. Probably, that little boy up to the time He was twelve years old called Joseph "father." However, Jesus was no longer a child; He had reached adolescence. "And he said unto them, 'How is it that ye sought me? Know ye not that I must be about my Father's business?'" (Luke 2:49). In other words, Jesus said, "Mother, you should have known. It wasn't necessary to look for me." Up to twelve years of age, when Joseph said, "Go and get that two-by-four," little Jesus ran and got the two-by-four. But He is twelve now; He has reached the age of adolescence, the age when He has a will and mind of His own. He says now, "I must be about my Father's business." Up to this point, He had been taught the Word of God, but I am not sure if He ever had been asked to make any kind of decision. But at twelve years of age, He said in effect, "I am now ready to assume my responsibility. From now on, I am about my Father's business." The will of Jesus is now bent to the will of God. What will He do? When I was thirteen years old, I learned how to sell door to door to the automotive industry in East St. Louis. I was being groomed for the family business too just like Jesus. "When you get old enough to make your own living and you don't eat here at my table or sleep in my bed, then you will make your own decisions. Until then, you will do what I tell you to do." He was a regular old meanie, wasn't he? Yet I attribute the firmness of my father to be one of the factors that kept me out of jail.

Now we see Jesus at the time of adolescence. What will He do? Leave home? Go out on His own? Is He going to start running a gang? No. He will do His Father's business, His Father's will. What is His Father's will? We read on: "And he went down with them, and came to Nazareth, and was subject unto them" (Luke 2:51).

As long as He is a teenager, He is subject to His parents. Such is His Father's will. Modern psychology has gotten us into terrible difficulty by running counter to this principle. Then we come again to Dr. Luke's notation in his physician's chart that covered the period from the beginning of adolescence to manhood:

"And Jesus increased in wisdom and stature, and in favor with God and man" (Luke 2:52). He increased in wisdom mentally— the one who is omniscient grew in wisdom. He increased in stature physically, growing as any other boy grows. He increased in favor, in grace, with God and man. That is spiritual growth. In all three areas of His total personality as a human being, He grew normally from the time He was twelve years old until He came to manhood. He grew mentally, physically, and spiritually during that period. My friend, a child who does not grow in all three areas will surely have trouble growing later on. Many letters come to my desk from folk newly saved. They ask questions that to you would sound stupid. But they are not stupid; they are baby questions that should have been answered in their teens. Someone failed to give them the scriptures when they were young. I wish we could visit that carpenter shop in Nazareth. I see a little boy around there helping His dad. I see Him at sixteen, seventeen, eighteen. Then at some time during His young years, Joseph probably died, and I see Jesus assuming the responsibility for which He had been prepared.

And he came to Nazareth, where he had been brought up; and, as his custom was, he went into the synagogue on the Sabbath day, and stood up to read. And there was delivered unto him the book of the prophet, Isaiah. And when he had opened the book, he found the place where it was written, The Spirit of the Lord is upon me, because he hath anointed me to preach the gospel to the poor; he hath sent me to heal the brokenhearted, to preach deliverance to the captives, and recovering of sight to the blind, to set at liberty them that are bruised, to preach the acceptable year of the Lord. And he closed the book, and he gave it again to the minister, and sat down. And the eyes of all them that were in the synagogue were fastened on him. And he began to say unto them, This day is this scripture fulfilled in your ears. And all bore him witness, and wondered at the gracious words which proceeded out of his mouth. And they said, 'Is not this Joseph's son?' (Luke 4:16–22)

## "Jesus Takes His Place"

His hometown was not large; everybody knew Him. As He grew up, they had recognized in Him only a normal boy-that is all. When He came to manhood and began His ministry, He came back to their synagogue and read to them the scriptures. They were amazed and said, "Why, this is Joseph's boy!" That is not all. He not only read to them that day but, oh, how He spoke to them. Resentment arose in their hearts.

"And all they in the synagogue, when they heard these things, were filled with wrath, and rose up, and thrust him out of the city, and led him unto the brow of the hill on which their city was built, that they might cast him down headlong. But he, passing through the midst of them, went his way" (Luke 4:28 -30).

His hometown mobbed Him at the beginning of His ministry. If it had been possible, they would have killed Him. Why? Well, they said, "We know Him. This is Joseph's boy and listen to Him talk!" At this time, He was thirty years of age, and He was perfectly human.

## "Jesus The Man Begins His Ministries"

Will you notice that when our Lord gave those wonderful mystery parables recorded in Matthew, the reaction of the public was the same? "Is not this the carpenter's son?" (Matthew 13:55). And when Mark was recording it, he got another remark, "Is not this the carpenter?" (Mark 6:3). When Jesus walked out at thirty years of age and began His ministry, the comment was not "He is a theologian" or "He is a scribe" or "He is a great religious leader." They said, "He is a carpenter!" May I digress to say that labor has never been reached with the Gospel since the industrial revolution. That is unfortunate, but it is true. In the early days, when the Gospel first started down the Roman road, slaves and poor folk were those who first came to Christ. Paul could say, "Not many wise . . . not many mighty, not many noble are called; but God hath chosen the foolish . . . the weak . . . and base things" (1 Corinthians 1:26–28). As far as I can tell, no effort is being made today to reach labor. Christianity unfortunately has been labeled "capitalism's religion." I have read that Calvinism was responsible for our present system of capitalism in this country. I think that is accurate, and it is good, but I think it is unfortunate that labor has been bypassed. And it is a strange development, for Jesus was a carpenter for thirty years. He knew what hard work was. The politician speaks of the calloused hands of toil. I am weary of politicians who are millionaires. He who has been born with a silver spoon in his mouth, whose soft hands never have been soiled by earning one day's living, does not know my problem. When a head of government talks of hours, man. Oh, to look in at Nazareth. You say He is a great teacher. Yes. But during those silent years, He was a good carpenter too. I rejoice in His manhood. He is my Lord and my God, but He was a man, a laboring man. We have looked now at a physician's chart, and we have heard the public's comment. Now let us look at the prophet's copy.

## "The Prophet's Copy"

The prophet is David, and his copy is Psalms 69. Some say that David is writing of his own experience in this psalm. He is, yet it is not only the experience of David, for he could never adumbrate all that is said here. This is a Messianic psalm. In the New Testament, it is quoted eleven times as referring to Christ. It is all about Him. In fact, this psalm is quoted more than any other, with the exception of Psalms 22, the great psalm of the crucifixion. As I read Psalms 69, I have the feeling that it relives the earthly experience of the Lord Jesus. As He hung on the cross, His suffering intensified by the beating sun and the jeering and ridicule being flung in His face;

His mind (perhaps in delirium) went back over His entire life.

## "Heads to Nazareth"

We begin with Him way up north at Nazareth. We hear the heart sob of a little boy, a teenager, a young man: "Save me, O God; for the waters are come in unto my soul. I sink in deep mire, where there is no standing; I am come into deep waters, where the floods overflow me. I am weary of my crying. My throat is dried; mine eyes fail while I wait for my God" (Psalms 69:1–3).

## "You and Your Silent Years"

If you will let those silent years speak to you, it will be a roar in your ears. Listen to Him: "O' Israel I am become a stranger unto my brethren, and an alien unto my mother's children" (Psalms 69:8).

Notice that it was not His father's but His mother's children. You see, Mary had other children. Perhaps one day, her boys, Judas and Joses, said to her, "Mother, we heard somebody down the street talking, and they said that Jesus is not really our brother. They said that nobody knows who His father is." Someone has said that God made the country, man made the city, but the devil made the small town. I believe that. If you have lived in a small town, you know that a little town can be cruel. What shall I do? "Do you know what was the matter? A little town like this will not accept you. I advise you to go to a city and start all over again where you are not known." Nazareth was a little town that would not accept the Lord Jesus because it would not believe the fact that He was the Son of God.

"I made sackcloth also my garment; and I became a proverb to them" (Psalms 69:11).

This one who was the stalwart carpenter of Nazareth made sackcloth His garment and was ridiculed to the point of becoming a proverb, a byword.

"They that sit in the gate speak against me, and I was the song of the drunkards" (Psalms 69:12).

Those who were sitting in the gate were the high officials of the town, the judges. Thus, we see that the best people in Nazareth also spoke against Him.

Down on skid row, they made up dirty little ditties and sang them about Him and His mother. I'm sure you can imagine what name they used for Him—it's still in the vocabulary of the present hour. That is what they called Him in Nazareth. My friend, this is the reason I cannot follow the crowd that denies the virgin birth, for to do so would be to join the Nazareth crowd in name calling. "But as for me, my prayer is unto thee, O LORD . . . Thou hast known my reproach, and my shame, and my dishonor; mine adversaries are all before thee. Reproach hath broken my heart, and I am full of heaviness; and I looked for someone to take pity, but there was none; and for comforters, but I found none" (Psalms 69:13, 19, 20).

"Wherefore, in all things it behooved him to be made like his brethren, that he might be a merciful and faithful high priest in things pertaining to God, to make reconciliation for the sins of the people. For in that he himself hath suffered being tempted, he is able to help them that are tempted" (Hebrews 2:17).

He not only perfectly understands you, but He loves you, and He stands ready to be your Savior. This one who is very God and very man was "despised and rejected of men" (Isaiah 53:3).

In those silent years, I see a young man growing normally in Nazareth; I hear the sound of a carpenter's hammer; I hear the sob of His soul. He is my Savior. He is my God. Is He yours?

# CHAPTER 7

# THE SILENT YEARS OF CHRIST

In fact, as we think about the carpenters that lived in Israel in Bible times, let us think about our Lord Jesus Christ. The Bible says that when it came time for Him to be born of the virgin, Mary, He was born into a family that was very familiar with carpentry. In fact, the stepfather of our Lord Jesus Christ, Joseph, was a carpenter in the city of Nazareth, in the province of Galilee. The Lord Jesus Christ, therefore, was raised in a carpenter's family.

## "Trade Passed On"

It was a custom among the Jews of the first century to teach their sons the skills that the father in the family had. So probably, somewhere around the age of fifteen, the Lord Jesus Christ began to learn from His stepfather, Joseph, the skills involved in being a carpenter. There was a saying among the Jewish men in the nation of Israel: "If you do not teach your son how to work, you teach him how to be a thief." So in all probability, about the age of fifteen, Jesus Christ began learning carpentry skills from His stepfather, Joseph.

As we read through the sermons of Jesus, there are many references to things that a carpenter would think about. For example, Jesus spoke about the "narrow gate" that we have to go through. You can imagine Him thinking about various gates that He had made along with His stepfather, Joseph. He talked about building a house "upon the rock" and not "upon the sand," another concept that a good first-century carpenter would have known about. In a beautiful passage, in Matthew 11:29, Jesus said that His "yoke" was easy. Based on His carpentry skills, He could make a yoke that was comfortable for the animals. In Matthew 21:33, He talked about building a tower in a vineyard. In another place, He told the parable of a king who was going to build a tower but did not count the cost. And you can just see the mind of a carpenter working there. You have to know the expenses before you begin a project such as that. Jesus spoke about the chief "cornerstone." And in Matthew 13:55, He is referred to as "the son of a carpenter."

But I would like to skip ahead from the time in which He worked as a carpenter to the time that He began His public ministry. There were two occasions where Jesus went back to His hometown of Nazareth and preached there to the people. One occasion was in Luke, chapter 4. And as he began to preach to the people there, from Isaiah, chapter 61, at first the people were just overwhelmed with the message that Jesus was giving them. But then, they became upset at Him, and they reached the point where they were angry at Him, and they tried to kill Him before He was able to leave town on that occasion.

But there was another time where our Lord Jesus went back to His hometown, again to preach to the people, and their reaction this time was similar to what happened the first time; that is, at first, they were overwhelmed by what He was saying, but then they got upset. And on this second occasion, what upset them was the fact that they knew that He was a carpenter.

Would you look with me please at Mark 6? I want to read verses 1 to 6, as the Lord returned to His hometown of Nazareth. Notice the reaction of the people as He began preaching.

"And He went out from there and He came into His hometown and His disciples followed Him. And when the Sabbath had come, He began to teach in the synagogue and many listeners were astonished, saying, "Where did this man get this knowledge? And what is this wisdom given to Him, and such miracles, as these performed by His hands? Is not this the carpenter? The son of Mary and the brother of James and Joses and Judas and Simon? And are not His sisters here with us?' And they took offense at Him. And Jesus said to them, 'A prophet is not without honor except in His hometown, and among His own relatives, and in His own household.' And He could do no miracle there except that He laid His hands upon a few sick people and healed them. And He wondered at their unbelief."

## "Silent Years Continue"

Notice again, back in verse 3, that after initially being enthralled with His message, they said to themselves, "Isn't this the carpenter, the son of Mary?" And based on that, they came to where they rejected Jesus Christ. Well, apparently, Jesus was not ashamed of being a carpenter from the age of 12 Years to 30 Years, when His public ministry began. I would like to ask you to think with me for a few moments about the significance of the fact that Jesus Christ served as a carpenter actually much longer than He ever served as a preacher. There are several attributes that are very significant about His profession as being a carpenter. Number one, the fact that he was a carpenter for those eighteen years emphasizes that God respects all honorable work that we might do, even manual labor, as a carpenter would have been engaged in. That, in itself, was a hard lesson for the Jews to learn, in the city of Nazareth. Jesus did not meet their concept of being the Messiah because He had been a carpenter from the age of twelve on up.

They expected the Messiah to be born in a palace. He wasn't; He was born in a cave. They expected Jesus to be born into a royal family. He wasn't; He was born by the virgin, Mary, with His stepfather, Joseph. They expected Jesus to be raised and to be taught military skills. What they really thought was the Messiah would be trained as a soldier, that ultimately, He would raise an army. He would be the general of that army, and based on that military power, He would force the Romans out of Judea. He would then become a king and establish the Jewish nation in Palestine. That was the Jewish view of the Messiah early in the first century.

## "No Silver Spoon"

But it didn't happen that way. He wasn't born in a palace to a royal family. He was not trained as a soldier or a military leader. He was trained to be a carpenter. Why? Because He wanted to identify Himself with the common people. He wanted to identify Himself with the dignity of manual labor. He wanted us to understand that as long as it is honest work that we are engaged in, then any job is respectable in the eyes of God. That is not the way the people of Nazareth saw being a carpenter. They were prejudiced here against those who worked with their hands. "Is this not the carpenter?"

Notice, in verse 3, they continued by saying, "Is this not the carpenter, the son of Mary?" Some people say, "Well, Joseph must have died by this point," and that is very possible; nevertheless, they could have said, "Is this not the son of Mary and the late Joseph?" What we see here is that they were continuing to insult Christ by assuming that He was illegitimate. That's why Joseph is not mentioned in verse 3. Not only did they look down on Him for being a carpenter, but they assumed that He was born illegitimately and not of the virgin, Mary. Jesus, therefore, chose being a carpenter because He wanted to demonstrate the dignity of manual labor.

When I was growing up, my dad used to say to my sister and me that he didn't care what we did in life. We could even become garbage men (or women); we could even pick up garbage for a living, as long as it was honest work and as long as we remained faithful to God. That is exactly what I have taught my children as they grew up in our household. It doesn't matter what you do in life, as long as it is honest work and as long as you remain faithful to God. I think that is what Jesus is telling us here, by choosing carpentry as His profession for these early years of His adult life. Any profession can be carried out for the glory of God.

There's a tombstone over in Great Britain. And on the tombstone, there is an epitaph written for a man who died, who was buried there. The man's name was Thomas Cobb. I want to read what that tombstone says: "Here lies Thomas Cobb, who mended shoes to the glory of God, for 40 years." What a great statement that is. We can mend shoes for a living. We can write musical compositions for a living as Johann Sebastian Bach did; and on every piece that he wrote, he put the letters SDG, which stood for "Sola Deo Gloria"—to God alone be the glory. Whether it is manual labor, whether it is mental labor, whether we are involved in some kind of other profession, we can still glorify God with the kind of work that we do.

Let's think of something else that is significant about Christ as a carpenter, and that is the nature of His work as a carpenter. What kind of work does a carpenter do? There are really two things that a carpenter does. He repairs things, and he builds things from scratch. Think about those two parts of a carpenter's job. In the first place, many times we call a carpenter to repair something that has become broken. Maybe a chair has a broken leg or the kitchen table has broken, and we need that wood repaired. Sometimes, there may be a big storm that comes through, and there's a giant tree that falls across the roof of the house and caves it in. Who do we call? We call the best team of carpenters that we can find. We want them to repair the damage. In the same way, Jesus Christ was a spiritual carpenter. People brought to Him their broken lives, and He was able to repair them just as He does today.

A few moments ago, we sang Number 62: "Bring Christ your broken life, so marred by sin. He will create anew, make whole again. Your empty wasted years, He will restore, and your iniquities, remember no more." Beloved, the great carpenter can look down upon us and see what messes we have made of our lives. He can take that mess we've made, that awful mistake that we committed, and He can begin to repair the damage and allow the healing to start. There's a beautiful verse that maybe we overlook sometimes along these lines. It's Matthew 12, verse 20, talking about Jesus Christ. The Bible says this, "A battered reed, He will not break off; and a smoldering wick, He will not put out." That's very interesting. Here is a reed out here that maybe the wind has bent over, and it's about to break off and to die. The Bible says that Jesus does not go out there and stomp on that thing and break it off, so it goes ahead and dies. He doesn't do that. "A broken reed, He will not break off; and a smoldering wick, He will not put out."

Here's a lamp that has a wick in it, and it's burned down, and the wick is just about to go out. Jesus Christ does not go over there and blow it out. He doesn't do that. In a spiritual sense, which is what the verse is referring to (Matthew 12:20), we look at our lives, and we see, many times, we are like that broken reed. I mean, we're just about ready to leave this life through despair, through depression, through all of the mistakes that we have made, and Christ does not go over and stomp on us.

And many times, we are like the smoldering wick. We're just at the bottom of life. Everything that can happen to us has happened. We have been defeated by life. But He does not go over and blow that little flame out. The great carpenter begins to work with that reed and that little flame and begins to rebuild our lives if we will let Him. Christ, therefore, as a carpenter, repairs our lives and doesn't just go ahead and allow us to suffer in misery.

There's a second thing that a carpenter does: he builds new items. Jesus is the great carpenter because John 1:3 says, "All things came into being by Him, and apart from Him, nothing came into being that has come into being." Can you imagine a carpenter who has built the universe? And yet that's what the Bible says. Everything that has been created was made by this carpenter. In the first century, Jesus was still building. He said,

"Upon this rock I will build My church, and the gates of Hades shall not overpower it."

On the day of Pentecost, in Acts 2, here's the great carpenter who built His church and brought it into existence and put it into service. Did you know the Bible tells us that Jesus is still a carpenter today? There's something that He is still working on today. In John 14:2, He said, "In My Father's house are many dwelling places, if it were not so, I would have told you; for I go to prepare a place for you." As the great carpenter, He is constructing places for us that we will dwell in once we reach heaven.

So we see that He was a carpenter in the sense that He repairs things—our lives. And He also builds things from scratch. There's a third idea that is significant when we consider Christ as a carpenter. And that is, how does a carpenter think? When a carpenter sees a piece of wood, how does he look at that piece of wood? Well, the answer is he sees it differently from the way most other people see the wood. Most people would look at a piece of wood out here and say, "Well, it's got all these knots in it. It's got cracks in it. It's got some ink on it where they stamped it at the lumberyard," and maybe it's bowed a little and so forth. A carpenter doesn't look at wood that way. The carpenter sees the potential that the wood has. A carpenter says, "Well, I can glue those knots back in. In some cases, that crack can be fixed, and that warp can be taken out with a plane or joiner," and various other imperfections can be worked out. The carpenter sees the potential of the wood, not the problems of the wood.

A carpenter, therefore, sees the potential in that wood and not the flaws and imperfections that might doom it in the eyes of others. Beloved, the great carpenter is still working with us today. He knows which tools to use on us to bring out our potential. He knows when maybe we need to be sanded down, and He carries that out. He knows when maybe we need to be polished, and He carries that out. He knows when various other things need to be done in our lives to bring out the talents that we have, and He carries those things out, if we will allow Him to do so. He sees our potential and works on that.

There's a final way in which Jesus, as a carpenter, is significant to us today, and this is in the manner of His death. The Lord Jesus Christ could have chosen to die in a number of ways. He could have chosen to be beheaded, as was John the Baptist. He could have chosen to be stoned to death, as they were in the old law of Moses, but He didn't choose to be stoned or to be beheaded. He could have chosen to be shot to death with an arrow, as was King Ahab, back in the Book of 1 Kings, chapter 22. But instead, He chose to die a carpenter's death because the Roman soldiers took a hammer and nails, the tools of a carpenter. The great carpenter, therefore, demonstrates the value of honest work. He demonstrates the fact that He can repair lives and build things from scratch. He demonstrates that He can see the potential that we have, as we ought to see potential in one another, and that He can work with us. And it also shows that He died a carpenter's death on a wooden cross.

I hope that some of these things have encouraged you. If you are not a member of the body of Christ, then please think about the fact that the carpenter died for you and for your sins. And as He bled to death upon the wooden cross, He was bleeding to death for your sins as well as those who have already obeyed the Gospel. We would urge you, therefore, to believe in Christ, to repent of your sins, to make the good confession, then to be baptized by immersion in water for the forgiveness of your sins, and enter in to the family of the great carpenter.

Because our faith is based upon a historical figure for whom more evidence exists than for Julius Caesar. Christians, Jews, journalists, theologians, historians, and skeptics all take an active interest in every archaeological or manuscript discovery that might shed light or doubt on the origins of our faith. We too must be armed with these facts to confirm our faith and equip ourselves with reasons for the faith we hold in order to answer enquirers (1 Peter 3:15).

During the nineties, many articles have been published identifying Jesus as a Jew, a Christian, an Essene, a politically correct socialist, a Buddhist, and most recently a Freemason. In March–April 1996 alone, several articles in major newspapers and periodicals were published concerning the historical figure of Jesus. Many of these covered the recent find of inscribed burial caskets from the first century. In one tomb were found the names of Jesus, Mary, and Joseph, another Mary (suggested to be Mary Magdalene), a Matthew, and a Juda, son of Jesus. Inevitably, this led to speculation that Jesus had not been raised from the dead, which was in contrast to a survey that showed that half of Britain still believed in the resurrection, more than four times the adult church-going population. TIME magazine recently ran a cover story entitled "The Search for Jesus: What Are Christians to Believe?" In these pages, we will do just that, search for the real Jesus, the "Christian" God and Jewish man "in one agreed."

The Bible itself has a high view of literal historical narrative, all of it was written for our instruction (Romans 15:4; 1 Corinthians 10:11). Therefore, we can be instructed out of the historical life of Jesus as much as from his definitive theological statements about God. We will derive faith from history rather than divide faith from history.

## "Jesus Was Raised a Jew"

From his birth, as is indicated by his very Jewish genealogy, Jesus was raised a Jew. He was circumcised the eighth day (Luke 2:21), bore a common Jewish name, Yeshua, "he [God] saves" (Matthew 1:21). In fact, Yeshua was the fifth most common Jewish name. Four out of the twenty-eight Jewish high priests in Jesus's time were called Yeshua. Joseph was the second most common male name and Mary the most common amongst women. This in itself is sufficient evidence to throw doubt on the recently found tomb of "Jesus, Mary, and Joseph," as it is like finding the gravestone of Mr. and Mrs. John Smith. In passing, it is worth noting that we do not know for sure if Jesus was born in a stable surrounded by animals, only that he was laid in a feed trough. In fact, Justin Martyr in the middle of the second century said that it was in a cave that Jesus was born owing to their being "no room at the inn" (Luke 2:7). That this story was widely believed (e.g., by Origen and the Apocryphal Gospels) is evident from the fact the Constantine had a church built on the site of the cave in the fourth century.

After his birth, Jesus was presented to the Lord in the Jerusalem temple (Luke 2:22; cf. Deuteronomy 18:4; Exodus 13:2, 12, 15) according to Mary's period of uncleanness (Leviticus 12:2–8). A sacrifice was offered for him—a pair of doves and two young pigeons—which indicated that his family were not wealthy (Leviticus 12:2, 6, 8; Luke 2:22–24). Thus, Jesus was raised according to the law (Luke 2:39).

## "Jesus and Jewish Education"

During the so-called missing years filled in by spurious Apocryphal Gospels, Jesus undoubtedly received a Jewish education perhaps along these lines: "at 5 years of age," he would be "ready for the study of the written Torah, at 10 years of age for the study of the Oral Torah . . . at 20 for pursuing a vocation, at 30 for entering one's full vigour." Interestingly, Jesus did just that, entering his ministry at about thirty years of age. Also, at thirty, a Jewish father might publicly declare his son to be the inheritor of all that he had or an adopted son in his place. The voice that spoke out of heaven at Jesus's baptism (Luke 3:22) was God declaring Jesus to be His true son and inheritor.

The Jews of Jesus's era were world innovators in comprehensive universal education. The majority, if not all, were taught to read and write. The philosopher Seneca remarked that the Jews were the only people who knew the reasons for their religious faith, something which the apostle Peter continued to commend (1 Peter 3:15). We often reflect on how Christianity was the initiator behind much of our modern education system, yet that motivation derives from its Jewish educational foundations.

The remark of a contemporary Jewish rabbi was that education began at six, and from then on, we "stuff him [with scriptural teaching] like an ox." Jesus only needed to hint at scriptural verses for his hearers to recollect the whole contexts in their minds. Their minds worked like Strong's Concordances. The scriptural knowledge of most Jewish children then would have surpassed that of most church leaders now. Nevertheless, it was faith and application that God was looking for. Lessons began with the Book of Leviticus at age five or six and progressed onward. Higher education began at fifteen when one would embark on theological discussion with learned teachers or rabbis.

By the age of twelve, we know that Jesus was growing in understanding as he was found in the temple precincts "both listening and asking questions" (Luke 2:46). The contemporary method of teaching included questioning to elicit intelligent responses, so Jesus's asking of questions may not have been just to obtain knowledge but also to teach it. Indeed, "they were astonished at his understanding and answers."

The study of Greek in Palestine in Jesus's day was not encouraged, although it was a necessity of daily life in the diaspora lands outside of Palestine. Greek philosophy was equally deprecated in Palestine. Early church theologians were later to remark "what has Athens to do with Jerusalem" decrying Greek thinking synthesis with Christian doctrine. It is unfortunate in the least that even in the church, New Testament Greek is studied in preference to Hebrew and the Greek classics instead of Jewish writings such as the Talmud and Mishnah.

## "Outward Form"

On the outside, Jesus even looked like a Jew. Certainly, being faithful to the law, he wore the tsîtsith ("tassel," Numbers 15:37-41; Matthew 9:20; 14:36; Luke 8:44. In English, these are obvious by the translations "hem" or "fringe of his garment," which the crowds were keen to touch in order to be healed).

He may also have worn the tephillin ("phylacteries," Deuteronomy 6:8), small boxes bound to arm and head containing the scriptural verses: Exodus 13:1–16, Deuteronomy 6:4–9 and 11:13–21. Jesus only criticized the exaggerating of these for ostentatious exhibitionism (Matthew 23:5), a practice also condemned by later rabbis. Conventionally, these were meant to be discreet, and the arm one was invisible under clothing. A rabbinic source suggests that the head one should only be worn in winter under a headband and not in summer when it would have been conspicuous. Actually, Edersheim thinks it unlikely that Jesus wore them. The practice was not universal in Jesus's time and not literally required from a reading of Deuteronomy 6:8.

## "Religious Attendance"

Every year (perhaps the family was prospering or were particularly dutiful for most only went up to Jerusalem occasionally), Jesus's family went up to Jerusalem to celebrate Passover (Pesach) (Luke 2:41-43), a tradition that Jesus continued (John 12:12; Mark 14:12-26). Jesus also kept tabernacles (Sukkôth, "booths:) (John 7:1-39). John 10:22-23 may also indicate that Jesus celebrated the Hanukkah festival, which commemorated the second century BC rededication of the temple under the Maccabees.

"As was his custom," he also attended synagogue every Sabbath (Luke 4:16) even during his travelling ministry (Mark 1:39; Matthew 4:23; 9:35; Luke 4:15, 16–27, 44).

## "Religious Observance"

In tithing, fasting, and almsgiving, he was totally Jewish. Although he opposed excessive worrying about the minutiae of tithing "mint, dill and cumin" (Matthew 23:23), he still argued that the crowds and his disciples should do as the scribes and Pharisees said (Matthew 23:3; "but not as they do"). In fact, the law only specified tithing of grain, wine, oil, and livestock.

Jesus said grace or rather a blessing before and/or after meals (Deuteronomy 8:10; Matthew 6:41; 26:26; and Luke 24:30, which is post resurrection; cf. Didache 10:1). The object of the blessing was not the food but God, when the New Testament inserts "it" or "the bread" in such verses. It is not found in Greek. It was inconceivable that a Jew would bless the object and not the originator/creator. The traditional blessing is: "Barukh attah 'Adonai 'elohenu Melekh ha-olam ha-motsi lechem meen ha-arets." ("Blessed are You, our Lord God, King of the Ages/Universe, who brings forth bread from the earth.")

In every respect, therefore, Jesus was a Jew and was not ashamed to call himself one: "We know what we worship, for salvation is from the Jews" (John 4:22).

Copyright © 1998 Jonathan Went. Used by permission.

Jonathan Went teaches at Christ for England Bible School and tutors Hebrew privately and by correspondence. He is a graduate of University College London. He has studied theology with London Bible College and is researching a PhD on the Hebrew nature of man. He resides in Norwich, England.

## Select Bibliography

David Friedrich Strauss, Das Leben Jesu, 1835–1836

Joseph Ernest Renan, Vie de Jésus, 1860

*Martin Kähler, The So-Called Historical Jesus and the Historic Biblical Christ, 1896*

Schweitzer, Albert, The Quest for the Historical Jesus, A&C. Black, 1906/10

Bultmann, Jesus and the Word, NY: Scribner's, 1934

Ernst Käsemann, lecture: "The Problem of the Historical Jesus," 1953Günther Bornkamm, Jesus of Nazereth, 1956/60

*James M. Robinson, A New Quest of the Historical Jesus, 1959*

Jeremias, Joachim, The Problem of the Historical Jesus, Fortress Press, 1964

Xavier Léon-Dufour, SJ, The Gospels and the Jesus of History, Collins, 1968

D. Flusser, Jesus, Herder & Herder, New York, 1969

ed. McArthur, Harvey K., In Search of the Historical Jesus, SPCK, 1970

Geza Vermes, Jesus the Jew, London: Collins, 1973

*Maccoby, Hyam, Revolution in Judaea—Jesus & the Jewish Resistance, Ocean Books, 1973*

Wilson, Ian, Jesus: The Evidence, Pan, 1984

Schonfield, Hugh, The Essene Odyssey, Element, 1984

*Rabbi Harvey Falk, Jesus the Pharisee: A New Look at the Jewishness of Jesus, NY: Paulist Press, 1985*

*Mack, B. H., A Myth of Innocence: Mark and Christian Origins, Fortress Press, 1988*

Lindsey, Robert L., Jesus Rabbi & Lord, Cornerstone, 1990

*Crossan, J. D., The Historical Jesus: The Life of a Mediterranean Jewish Peasant, T&T Clark, 1991*

Wilson, A. N., Jesus, Sinclair Stevenson, 1992

Barbara Thiering, Jesus the Man, Doubleday, 1992

Wright, N. T., Who was Jesus? SPCK, 1992

E. P. Sanders, The Historical Figure of Jesus, Penguin Press: Allen Lane, 1993

*W. Hamilton's Quest for the Post-Historical Jesus*

E. Gruber and H. Kersten, The Original Jesus

C. Knight and R. Lomas, The Hiram Key

*Witherington III, Ben, The Jesus Quest—The third search for the Jew of Nazareth, Paternoster, 1995*

Shorto, Russell, Gospel Truth, Hodder&Stoughton, 1997

# Notes #

The Times, September 19, 1992 reporting on Jesus by A. N. Wilson. Also, The Times, October 9, 1993, reporting on the latest definition of Jesus in the New Shorter Oxford English Dictionary. #

A common misnomer, a Christian is someone who follows Christ. If Christ were a Christian, he would be following himself, like a dog chasing his own tail. #

A member of the Dead Sea Scroll community at Qumran, an apocalyptic Jewish sect. Suggested by Barbara Thiering's book Jesus the Man, Doubleday, 1992. Also, see Schonfield's The Essene Odyssey, Element, 1984 #

The Times, December 23, 1993, reporting on E. P. Sanders's The Historical Figure of Jesus *and W. Hamilton's Quest for the Post-Historical Jesus.* #

The Times, March 4, 1995, and The Sunday Times, April 2, 1995, reporting on The Original Jesus by E. Gruber and H. Kersten. #

The Sunday Times, April 7, 1996, reporting on The Hiram Key by C. Knight and R. Lomas. #

Reported on the BBC's Heart of the Matter, April 7, 1996. #

The Sunday Times, April 7, 1996, reporting on two separate surveys with figures of forty-eight to fifty percent for belief in the resurrection. #

TIME magazine, April 8, 1996. Also see the cover story: "Who was Jesus?" TIME magazine, August 15, 1988. #

Robert Funk of the Jesus Seminar quoted in the Los Angeles Times, February 24, 1994, View section #.

Schweitzer, Albert, The Quest for the Historical Jesus, A&C. Black, 1906/10, p. 4 #

English translation by the novelist George Eliot #

Bultmann, Jesus and the Word, NY: Scribner's, 1934, p #

Robert Funk of the Jesus Seminar quoted in the Los Angeles Times, March 5, 1989 #

The Times, October 21, 1994 #

Karl Adam from Tubingen; cf. Küng, Judaism #

The Times, January 14, 1995 #

Tony Higton, letter, in The Times, October 9, 1993 #

*Rabbi Harvey Falk, Jesus the Pharisee: A New look at the Jewishness of Jesus, NY, 1985, p.158* #

A. N. Wilson, Jesus, Sinclair Stevenson, 1992, p. 68 #

*Justin Martyr, Dialogue with Trypho the Jew, 78* #

The Times, November 12, 1997 #

A third-century Christian writer #

*Origen, Against Celsus, 6.36* #

cf. Vincent Taylor, Mark, p. 299f versus Cranfield, Mark, p. 194f #

Geza Vermes, Jesus the Jew, p. 21. Cf. D. Flusser, Jesus, Herder & Herder, New York, 1969,

p. 20; yYeb.9b; yKid.66a, bAZ 50b. #

Justin Martyr, a second-century Christian writer writing in Dialogue with Trypho the Jew, 88 #

Torah is the Hebrew word for instruction, teaching, law, and scripture itself. #

Mishnah, Avot, 5.21; the Mishnah is a collection of contemporary and later Jewish sayings #

Brought in during the first century BC and the first century AD #

Mishnah, Baba Bathra, 21a. #

A reason given for this is that Leviticus teaches on pure sacrifices, and the sacrifice of a child is pure. #

Mishnah, Aboth, 5.21 #

This is the literal meaning of keraia, the Greek word here. #

According to Papias, an early church bishop at the beginning of the second century #

Tertullian #

Mishnah, Baba Kamma, 83a #

Mishnah, Menachoth, 99b #

*Alfred Edersheim, The Life and Times of Jesus the Messiah, Vol. 1, p. 624–5 #*

A practice continued in the early church, cf. the Didache 13:5–7, an early church document.

## "Footnotes"

The silent years of Christ has been a time that so many religions would love to remove. In our research of well over 700 hours there is very little about Jesus Christ from the age of 12 to the age of 30. In the 1940's over 3000 books vanished by the hands of the Vatican. Why did they do this? What was the purpose of their deceit? We know that by 1948 the Acropha Gospels was removed from their canon. There are other religious sects that have made erroneous statements that Jesus Christ after Joseph died, was seen in India: The Buddhist religion would have us believe that Jesus became a Buddhist. Some would even say that he went to Persia and studied the Muslim religion. And then again that is a fallacy. The truth of the matter is, when the eldest son, at the loss of his father would have to provide, not only for his mother but also for his younger siblings. He would then have to remain with his family until the next younger boy would reach the age of 18. By this time Jesus would be 30 years of age and no longer accountable to his mother. Fact or Fiction? You decide.

## CHAPTER 8

# THE SAVIOR

*Behold the Lamb of God that taketh away the sins of the world. John 1:29*

## "Titles of the Savior"

*Behold the Lamb of God that taketh away the sins of the world. John 1:29*

There are many titles that Jesus has gone through in his walk for thirty-three and a half years.

"My Refuge and My Savior" (2 Samuel 22:3). God, the God of my rock. In him, will I trust. He is my shield and the horn of my salvation, my high tower, and my refuge, my savior. Thou savest me from violence.

## "Eight Things to Bear Witness To"

Isaiah 43:11: "I, even I, am the Lord, and beside me there is no savior." There are eight things that we need to bear witness to:

That I am He. That before Me, there was no God. That after Me, there will be no God formed. That I am Jehovah. That beside me, there is no other Savior. That I declared former things that have already come to pass. That I have saved you. That I have showed you things when no strange God among you could reveal them to you.

I am the only true eternal God, the first being, and I did not derive My existence from anyone else. I have not succeeded another, and My kingdom is the original underived and independent one. No one will ever succeed Me on My throne. I am Jehovah, and beside Me, there is no Savior. I have demonstrated by predictions, salvation, and miracles that I am God and you My witness.

## "The Redeemer Lives"

Thus says the Lord, the Redeemer of Israel and its Holy One, to the despised one, to the one abhorred by the nation, to the Servant of rulers, "Kings will see and arise. Princes will also bow down, because of the LORD who is faithful, the Holy One of Israel who has chosen You."

## "The Helper in Time of Trouble"

Thus says the Lord, "In a favorable time I have answered you. And in a day of salvation I have helped you. And I will keep you and give you for a covenant of the people, To restore the land, to make them inherit the desolate heritages."

This means that although He was God, He was also man and submitted to human laws and earthly rulers. Kings and princes will worship Him, which proves Him to be divine and Isaiah or some ordinary man and certainly not the church or Israel as some think.

As used here of the Messiah, it does not mean personal salvation from sin. It refers to hearing and helping Him in the day that God would be gracious and provide salvation for all men.

## "God Loves the Sinner but Hates the Sin"

You see, God makes it available to the Jew and the Gentile. The question is do you want it? The Bible says that all have sins and fall short of the glory of God (Romans 3:23). The wages of sin is death, but the gift of life is eternal through Christ Jesus (Romans 6:23).

The Bible is full of warnings with devastating results of rebellion and disobedience. The grim statistics in this world confirm the Bible scriptures.

Playing it fast and furious is dangerous business, and there is a price to pay. The price you pay for playing fast and furious occurs in psychological scars, social stigma, and alienation from God.

## "In the Last Days, Perilous Times Shall Come"

This is a high cost to low living and playing it fast and furious. St. Paul warned that "in the last days, perilous times shall come" (2 Timothy 3:1).

The word perilous speaks of a dangerous, violent, out-of-control society, and we see it all around us today. Only a very discerning or foolish person would not see the connection between today's current world events and the time-tested words of Jesus Christ. Only a foolish person would not see that we are now living in the last days, and "in the last days, perilous times shall come."

Violent motorcycle gangs and a host of other thugs rape, bomb, steal, and kill at will. Allegedly, even some police and judges are afraid of their threats. Everywhere in the world, the same problems exist. Recently, Belgium has been experiencing traumatic times as authorities there have discovered a string of child sex killings as pedophiles are on the loose. Prostitutes and transvestites have also been murdered. The whole world is involved in fighting and war, countries against countries and religions against religions. The Middle East war crisis is causing turmoil and fear in every person, and the words of the Bible have never been truer. "In the last days, perilous times shall come" (2 Timothy 3:1)

Sinners prostitute themselves. And at the same time, other sinners are killing prostitutes. Why? The wages of sin is death.

According to the Reader's Digest (April 1998) and other well-documented reports, the lighter-skinned fanatical Muslim extremists in Sudan have killed an estimated one million black Christians in that country since 1987. Blacks and Christian women and girls are sold as slaves for as little as thirty-five US dollars each, and these girls and women are being forced to convert to Islam or die.

## "The Wages of Sin Is Death"

The wages of sin is death. Why is this statement true? The price to pay for sin is death. Sinners kill and enslave. The carnage and killing is growing more each day worldwide, and it brings up images of the earlier slaughter in Zaire, Burundi, and Rwanda, where tribal hatred lay at the root of the genocide.

## "Evil and Sin Lurk Everywhere"

Evil and sin lurks everywhere, and along with it comes death. Only the Gospel of Jesus Christ is able to heal the hurts and to make a difference in a world full of sin, hatred, and murder.

Our world, our society is full of child abuse, sexual immorality, perversion, vicious muggings, brutal beatings, torturous disfigurement, a growing drug culture, deal dealing, AIDS, and cold-blooded murder.

## "These Are the Last Days and These Are Certainly Perilous Times We Live In"

Would you not say we are living in a time that could be described easily as "perilous times"? Again, the Bible scripture comes to mind: "in the last days, perilous times shall come" (2 Timothy 3:1).

Cruising homosexuals, lusty prostitutes, and loose-living high rollers are in a high-risk category to get hurt badly. Life in the fast and furious lane of sodomy, drugs, casual sex, and gambling is paying huge dividends. The dividends are trauma, suicide, murder, and death. The wages of sin is death.

## "Remember – The Wages of Sin Is Death"

Beautiful nineteen-year-old Lorelei Brose was found dead with a bullet in her head on a Sunday morning in a hotel room in Toronto a number of years ago.

She was a prostitute. Her close friends, also hookers, believe the killing could have been over a dispute about drugs, settling a score by a ripped-off customer or a message to Brose's pimp.

The dead girl's family told the sad story of a good girl gone bad. Just eighteen months earlier, Brose had left home to make a lot of money in prostitution. She wound up dead. The wages of sin is death, and in this case, it proved true.

More than a dozen hookers have been murdered in Toronto's downtown area this past decade. Among those investigated is the killing of Susan Anne Siegal, twenty, of Calgary, who was found strangled near the Ontario stockyards.

Hooking is dangerous business involving pimps, weird sicko clients, and AIDS-infected bisexuals.

About a decade ago, a sixteen-year-old Vancouver prostitute was diagnosed as having AIDS, Canada's first hooker to contract the deadly disease. In a number of African countries, ninety percent

of the prostitutes are infected with HIV and more than fifty percent with full-blown AIDS.

The constant threat of being infected with syphilis, gonorrhea, or genital herpes is also always present. And now there is chlamydeous (chlamydia), the sexually transmitted disease (STD) with the fastest-rising incidence, with three to four million new cases each year in the USA.

Altogether, physicians now know of at least twenty-five sexually transmitted diseases. These are diseases that are spread by sexual contact, whose effects can include sterility, cancer, chronic pain, problem pregnancies, abnormal children, and even death.

Male prostitutes who service with sodomy are very vulnerable and invite a horrendous death by the formerly called "gay plague."

## "The Wages of Sin Is Death"

Homosexual lovers of AIDS victim Rock Hudson have battled over his fifty-million-US-dollar will for years. Rock Hudson's secret boyfriend, Mark Christian, sought and received compensation in the millions of dollars because he did not know that Rock Hudson had the AIDS virus when they practiced sodomy together. The wages of sin is death, and Rock Hudson paid the high price of death for his sins.

There is freedom from "this hell that is homosexuality," says Torjus Fjagesund of Oslo, Norway, who was introduced to sodomy while in the army.

He writes: "Homosexuality is a complete and total perversion. It was not meant for a human being. It is the work of unclean spirits, yes and the devil himself. I was told that it was right for me, but it turned out to be a living hell. It's like being raped continually by the devil."

The next morning after receiving special prayer by people of God, I wakened a new man. I was one hundred ten percent man."

*Alcohol addiction is almost as bad, in the end. It's the civilized way to live but an awful way to die. Here again, we see the wages of sin is death.*

Alcohol causes cirrhosis of the liver, heart disease, bleeding ulcers, high blood pressure, and delirium tremens. And blackouts are some of its spinoffs.

My advice to social drinkers is "Stop now because if you keep on hitting the bottle, you surely will be sorry."

Sometime ago, I was confronted by a very drunk lady on the streets of Alesund, Norway, while walking to my hotel room after a revival service at the downtown church. She came waltzing out of a bar right into my path. Immediately, I said, "I am a pastor. May I help you." When she saw my clerical collar, she said, "Oh, you're one of those. I am not looking for a prayer meeting. I am looking for a party." I replied, "But I can help you."

She broke into tears, saying that she had been an airline stewardess with Scandinavian Airlines and was married to a fine, well-to-do man. She was living in a beautiful home, but alcohol had gotten a hold of her.

"Yes," she wanted help as she was very unhappy, she stated. Two years after retiring, her social drinking had progressed steadily into alcoholism, and her marriage was suffering. Then suddenly, she changed her mind and darted across the street through the traffic to a waiting taxi.

There is hope however. The same verse in the Bible that states, "The wages of sin is death" also declares "but the gift of God is eternal life through Jesus Christ our Lord."

Jesus Christ gives us the power to change. Yes, the wages of sin is death, but we are free to receive the gift of God, which is eternal life.

And remember, my friend, God is merciful and compassionate as well as all-powerful to deliver. God does not want you to sin, and He does not want you to pay for your sin with death. God wants for you to have eternal life.

The Bible says, "For God so loved the world, that He gave His only begotten Son, that whosoever believeth in Him should not perish, but have everlasting life" (John 3:16).

Here is Jesus's personal invitation: "Come unto Me, all ye that labour and are heavy laden, and I will give you rest" (Matthew 11:28).

## "God Loves a Soldier"

Each soldier must individually receive Jesus Christ as Savior and Lord; then we can know and experience God's love and plan for our lives.

We must receive Christ into our hearts as our Lord and Savior.

"As many as received Him, to them He gave the right to become children of God, even to those who believe in His name" (John 1:12).

God knows your heart and is not so concerned with your words as He is with the attitude of your heart. The following is a suggested prayer:

"Lord Jesus, I need You. Thank You for dying on the cross for my sins. I open the door of my life and receive You as my Savior and Lord. Thank You for forgiving my sins and giving me eternal life. Take control of the throne of my life. Make me the kind of person You want me to be."

Does this prayer express the desire of your heart? If it does, I invite you to pray this prayer right now, and Christ will come into your life, as He promised.

God would not only hear and help him but preserve and give over to the maker of a new covenant to the people to establish the earth and to restore and cause the waste places of the earth to be inhabited.

Christ did make a new covenant when he abolished the Mosaic contract, but it will not be made with Israel until the second coming of Christ after the rapture.

## "He Is Our Restorer"

"Surely My hand founded the earth, And My right hand spread out the heavens; When I call to them, they stand together.

"Assemble, all of you, and listen! Who among them has declared these things? The LORD loves him; he will carry out His good pleasure on Babylon, And His arm will be against the Chaldeans. "I, even I, have spoken; indeed I have called him, I have brought him, and He will make his ways successful. "Come near to Me, listen to this: From the first I have not spoken in secret, From the time it took place, I was there. And now the Lord GOD has sent Me, and His Spirit."

Thus says the Lord, your redeemer, the Holy One of Israel, "I am the LORD your God, who teaches you to profit, who leads you in the way you should go."

"If only you had paid attention to My commandments! Then your well-being would have been like a river, And your righteousness like the waves of the sea. Your descendants would have been like the sand, And your offspring like its grains; Their name would never be cut off or destroyed from My presence To restore the earth and cause desolate places to be inhabited."

The second time the loosing of prisoners is mentioned in Isaiah, it refers to the liberation of the righteous souls from sin when Christ was resurrected and ascended to heaven. This seems confirmed by the fact that loosing prisoners is followed by referring to life and death, both here and where the passage is quoted. These prisoners are spoken of as having the Messiah as their shepherd. He will feed in the ways along the paths in which he leads and guides them to the spring water.

### *"We Know That This is the Savior of the World – and Not of the Jews Only"*

Here are three things in which their faith grew: (1.) In the matter of it or that which they did believe. Upon the testimony of the woman, they believed him to be a prophet or some extraordinary messenger from heaven. But now that they have conversed with him, they believe that he is the Christ, the Anointed One, the very same that was promised to the fathers and expected by them and that, being the Christ, he is the Savior of the world. For the work to which he was anointed was to save his people from their sins. They believed him to be the Savior not only of the Jews but of the world, which they hoped would take them in, though Samaritans, for it was promised that he should be Salvation to the ends of the earth, (Isaiah 49:6). (2.) In the certainty of it, their faith now grew up to a full assurance: We know that this is indeed the Christ; alethos—truly, not a pretended Christ but a real one, not a typical Savior, as many under the Old Testament, but truly one. Such an assurance as this of divine truths is what we should labor after. Not only we think it probable and are willing to suppose that Jesus may be the Christ, but we know that he is indeed the Christ. (3.) In the ground of it, which was a kind of spiritual sensation and experience: Now we believe, not because of thy saying, for we have heard him ourselves. They had before believed for her saying, and it was well. It was a good step. But now they find further and much firmer footing for their faith: "Now we believe because we have heard him ourselves and have heard such excellent and divine truths, accompanied with such commanding power and evidence, that we are abundantly satisfied and assured that this is the Christ." This is like what the queen of Sheba said of Solomon (1 Kings 10:6, 7): The one half was not told me. The Samaritans, who believed for the woman's saying, now gained further light, for to him that hath shall be given. He that is faithful in a little shall be trusted with more. In this instance, we may see how faith comes by hearing. [1.] Faith comes to the birth by hearing the report of men. These Samaritans, for the sake of the woman's saying, believed so far as to come and see to come and make trial. Thus, the instructions of parents and preachers and the testimony of the church and our experienced neighbors recommend the doctrine of Christ to our acquaintance and incline us to entertain it as highly probable. But [2.] faith comes to its growth, strength, and maturity, by hearing the testimony of Christ himself. And this goes further and recommends his doctrine to our acceptance and obliges us to believe it as undoubtedly certain. We were induced to look into the scriptures by the saying of those who told us that in them, they had found eternal life. But when we ourselves have found it in them too, have experienced the enlightening, convincing, regenerating, sanctifying, comforting power of the word, now we believe, not for their saying but because we have *searched them ourselves. And our faith stands not in the wisdom of men but in the power of God.*

# CHAPTER 9

# THE POWER OF THE TALLITH

I was given a fringed blue-and-white prayer Shawl with the inscription of Hebrew Jardin. I heard that when Jesus wore the tallith miraculous and marvelous signs and wonders occur from heaven above. I never believed in magic or icons that would bring out the supernatural of a different kind. Yet something I believe is miraculous when the power of God showed up with Jesus as well as myself. I preached at many meetings and healing services by placing the Tallith on sick people. We saw cancer, heart conditions, aids and diabetes healed in Jesus name. There was even a pastor of a well-known church that the Tallith was placed on his head. He was anointed from the most high God.

## "The Miracles of Christ"

I was listening to a DJ on the radio talk about a man that went to the Mayo clinic in 2007 and had inoperable liver cancer and was told to go home and make arrangements for him to die. All his efforts were placed on the opinion of a man and not the great high physician. Imagine if this man had a miracle healing that he might be alive today.

## "Jesus Shows His Power"

A lot of people would have said that the power of the tallith showed up at the miracle of Cana which Jesus turned the water into wine. Many theologians, preachers, teachers and even philosophers would have said that it truly was a miracle. This story teller believes this first miracle of the power of the tallith was found at the temple in Nazareth. And this is how the dialogue would begin: A man in his late 50's or 60's stands up and asks for Jesus to read from the book of Isaiah, as the Sanhedrin looks on in awe. Jesus then responds by standing up. Son of Joseph and Mary you have our permission to read. Jesus approaches the pulpit and turns toward the Sanhedrin. He then takes his tallith, kisses the top where the inscriptions are and then places it on his head where it reaches from head to foot. The spirit of the Lord God is upon me: because the Lord hath anointed me to preach good tidings unto the meek: then Jesus looks up and smiles at seeing their reaction. He has sent me to bind up the broken hearted; to proclaim liberty to the captives, and the opening of the prison to them that are bound. To proclaim the acceptable year of the Lord, and the day of vengeance of our God to comfort all that mourn. He then closes the book and clasps his hands together and says: all scripture has been fulfilled this hour. He then walks away from the pulpit and sits in the High Priests' chair. The Sanhedrin with a disdain look on their brow, begin to mutter murmurings. Even one man in the back of the crowd said – stone him, stone him for he blasphemed God and the office of the High Priest. When they were arguing amongst themselves Jesus disappeared from their sight without their knowledge. He ended up at a well on the outskirts of Nazareth. You could say from that day forward the power of the tallith was in motion. Jesus saw a very elderly man that he recognized from his youth. He said, Rabbi as his hands covered the mans eyes and started walking out of Nazareth. The man screamed with a sense of enjoyment. Then for the first time in so many years he could now see. In his enthusi- asm for his new miracle he runs to the temple with a bated breath the man says, I'm healed, I'm healed, I'm healed. He raises his hands to heaven and says only God can heal. He is here and I have seen him. All of the Sanhedrin circles around him and he touches their face and recognizes them by name for the first time in many years.

I believe that the power of the tallith for the first time in Jesus was manifested. Jesus went about healing all those that were oppressed by the devil. Acts 10:38. To me, that is the first miracle. It's not the garment that heals, although many people have felt him in them. Jesus was God inside and a man on the outside.

## "We Are Just Vessels Used by God"

I have seen the power in God, not in man. We are just vessels being used to see God's glory magnified in these last days. I could give God the glory on so many miracles that he has performed through the power of the tallith. As a matter a fact, we could write many wonder tabloids that would still not convince the world about God's glory.

I went to my brother and his wife. She had an uncontrollable itch and my brother had a stint in his heart. He was afraid he would be leaving the world earlier than was expected. I placed first the tallith on her and instructed her to hold on to all four knots that represents the name of God. As she did that, the power of God hit her, and she went out in the spirit.

"Oh my gosh," she said, "you mean to tell me that God is in the power of the tallith, and you are not a Houdini?"

Then I placed the same tallith over my brother, and he was thrown four feet onto his couch. Since then, he has been a believer. It is said that is what we have to have happen to us to see God in our lives. Another man was in a meeting, and I put the tallith on him, and he was healed of cancer. He has suffered prostate cancer and breast cancer. It was the power of God on the tallith that made it possible. I told him that if you would just allow it to happen, you would see the signs and wonders that would follow. Peter's shadow is said to have healed those whom it touched as he passed by (Acts 5:15–16). Handkerchiefs and aprons that had touched Paul brought healing (Acts 19:11–12). I'm uncomfortable with all this because of our human tendency to worship and venerate people and objects who are not God. The Second Commandment is designed to prevent this: "You shall not make for yourself an idol in the form of anything in heaven above or on the earth beneath or in the waters below. You shall not bow down to them or worship them; for I, the Lord your God, am a jealous God" (Exodus 20:4–5).

## "The Tallith (Talit-Talitha) of Jesus Had Six Hundred Thirteen Fringes"

"Speak unto the children of Israel, and bid them that they make the fringes in the borders of their garments throughout their generations, and that they put upon the fringe of the borders a rib band of blue: And it shall be unto you for a fringe, that ye may look upon it, and remember all the commandments of the Lord, and do them; and that ye seek not after your own heart and your own eyes, after which ye use to go a whoring: That ye may remember, and do all my commandments, and be holy unto your God" (Numbers 15:38–40).

The outer garment of Jesus had six hundred thirteen fringes. When Jews saw these fringes, they were reminded:

Of the law of God.

They were responsible to obey the law of God.

They were called to be holy people.

Jesus wore an inner garment of lightweight material that extended to the wrists and ankles covered by an outer garment tied around the waist with a band of cloth and heavy leather sandals tied by leather thongs.

## "From Revealing Jewish Roots by Bill Morford"

The tallith (pronounced ta-leet') has been made without the blue thread in the fringe for centuries because the exact blue dye has not been available. The tallith is also called a prayer shawl because when it is pulled up over the head, it provides privacy and prevents distraction, allowing the wearer to pray as if going into a closet or tent.

Jesus said, "But when you pray, go into your private room (closet King James Version), and closing the door, pray to your Father who is in secret" (Matthew 6:6). The Greek word translated private room or closet is tameion, taken from the Hebrew word cheder, referring to the tallith as a prayer room or closet. Acts 18:3: "And because he (Paul) was a tentmaker as they (Priscilla and Aquila) were, he stayed and worked with them." The word tent maker in the King James Version is the Greek word skenopoios, meaning one that made small portable tents of leather, cloth, or linen. As previously stated, the tallith was also referred to as a tent. The Center of Judaic Christian Studies has found this reference in Israeli writings from around the first century. This particular reference to Paul, Priscilla, and Aquila is significant because we know that Paul had studied under Gamaliel (Acts 22:3) and that Priscilla and Aquila must also have been trained for Paul to have such high regard for their knowledge. Tying the knots on the fringes of a tallith was specialized, requiring rabbinical training. Every thread and every knot was significant. Some scholars feel that Paul, Priscilla and Aquila may have been tallith makers.

## "The First and Greatest Commandment"

Jesus said unto him, "Thou shalt love the Lord with all thy heart, and with all thy soul, and with all thy mind. This is the first and great commandment" (Matthew 22:37–38). The scribes had divided the six hundred thirteen commandments (which Jesus was required to know by age thirteen) into two hundred forty-eight affirmative commands to correspond with the members of the body and three hundred sixty-five negative commands to correspond with the days of the year.

# CHAPTER 10

# THE MYSTERY OF
# THE NUMBER 12

Over 7000 years ago when God was creating the earth for the second time, he aligned the stars. It says in Revelation 12 that the woman wore a crown on her head and that was the representation of the 9 planets and the 3 stars which is what made up the crown. Some people in todays society of Christianity have been looking for the sign of the rapture, so they use Revelation 12 as their guideline with their faith to show Jesus' return. That is not what God shows us in Revelation 12. Let's go back to the beginning of the 7000 years when God created Adam. We have 12 ribs in our bodies just like Adam did. This begins to unwind the mystery of the number 12. Later on, in Genesis we start to see from the 12 matriarchs another symbol of the 12. God starts to put together the 12 tribes that will make up the Jewish nation. Nothing compares to what happened at the time of Jesus Christ. It is almost like he had a purpose.

### "Jesus Encounters Simon"

Let's imagine you are Jesus and you were just tempted for 40 days and 40 nights and you returned back to Galilee. You see a bunch of fishermen and you approach a man in his mid 30's with worn down apparel and a scruffy beard with curly hair. You toss your bag on the side of the seashore and you walk into the water towards this man. The man is disgusted because he did not catch even one fish. This is how the dialogue begins.

As Jesus speaks to the man and Jesus says Simon, grab my hand so I can come in to your boat. Simon says, why are you coming into my boat? I told you I didn't get any fish and I am tired. Yet with Simons' inquisitive nature, he grabbed Jesus hand and pulled him into the boat. He says Simon, let's go out again for the last time. And as bewildered as Simon felt by Jesus statement, he begins to do exactly that. Simon sets his boat for departure. While on the middle of the Sea of Galilee where Simon just returned from with no luck, he takes the nets and throws them over the left side where he originally caught nothing. Jesus stops him and says to Simon, smiling, throw the nets over to the right side. As he is doing this, Jesus reaches down into the water and begins to stir the waters. His actions were favorable to the outcome. Simon begins to laugh out loud as he is drawing the nets into the boat he is amazed at all the fish now in the nets. He repeated the process over and over until he had 12 baskets of fish. As he reaches the maximum of his baskets, which is 12 baskets, he sets sail and says to Jesus – Who are you? Jesus grabs his leg with his left hand and says, I am Jesus. He also says to him, Simon come with me and I will make you a fisher of men. As the sun is setting and the fish are being taken off the ship by his crew and Simon says to the crew, I'm going with this man. Give the money to my wife and tell her that. And they depart and head into Jerusalem.

Now we start to see the mystery of the number 12 come to fruition. If Simon did not have the faith of the number 12 he would be disgusted and busted. Think of the sequence of events that would have occurred if Jesus had not been there at that time. We see that Simon, because of his prideful attitude and arrogance was doing it wrong. But when Jesus came in and straightened him out and put him on the right path he was doing everything right.

Jesus' purpose was to put together a ragtag group of men who were from all walks of life. They were fishermen, scribes, tax collectors, doctors and other various occupations. Then they walk with Jesus and noticed that he always had a goal in mind.

## "Five Loaves of Bread and Two Fishes"

We see the followers of Jesus begin to grow as they see all the signs, wonders and miracles performed by the Messiah as the word begins to get out. The boat with the 12 men are now headed to the island near the Sea of Galilee. When the boat comes to shore Jesus hears the noise of 5-10,000 people on the shore as he jumps out of the boat ahead of the apostles.

Simon says, Jesus they have all come here to hear you speak, but how are we going to feed all of them. Jesus says to Simon, see what we have and bring it to me. Now all the disciples of Jesus have left the boat and are greeted by all the people. As Simon notices a little boy with a fishing pole over his back and carried a basket of 2 fishes and 5 loaves of bread. Simon says to the boy, little boy my master is in need of the fishes and bread. And the little boy says to him, these fish are for my father and mother and if I give them to you they will have none. That is when Jesus put his hand on the heart of the little boy and he gladly gave the fish and bread to Jesus. Jesus said to Simon, please break them up into groups of 50 people and take your brothers along to help you. Then Jesus took the fish and raised the basket to heaven, and bellows – all you have to have is faith and believe and you will receive. When the basket was lowered it was overflowing and the crowd began to cheer excessively. Then Simon and the Apostles began to give out the fish and the fish began to multiply. Everyone received fish and the basket was never empty. Jesus also put the bread up to Heaven and it also multiplied and all the people were fed with the bread. And when everyone was fed, Jesus motioned to the Apostles to go inside the boat and pull out 11 more baskets and they did so. There were 12 baskets of loaves and fishes that were left after all were fed. As the little boy thanked Jesus and Jesus appointed 12 people to carry the 12 baskets to the boys' home.

Again, we see the mystery of the number 12 being used by Jesus. Where was their faith? At first it diminished. Instead of listening to the bread of life that was the word of God, man is always looking at his belly. But by faith, God provided as he always does. Again, another miracle from God. Then Jesus went to the top of the mount and began to preach and everyone was at awe at what they heard. As the physicians and the sagasies looked on to find fault in Jesus, Jesus and the 12 apostles depart and head over across the sea. While crossing over the sea, Jesus decides to go to sleep. While sleeping a storm begins to brew. As all the apostles begin to be frightened and the water starts to rush in as they begin to take down their sail Jesus reaches to Heaven with his right hand and says – Be Still. The apostles look on in awe as the seas become calm and the skies begin to become bright. Simon says to them, look he even controls the seas and the storms. They put up the sails and headed to the other side to Galilee.

## "12 Leagues of Demons"

As the apostles approach the other side of the island in the boat, Jesus steps out of the boat again with a purpose. It is like every wrong had to be righted. Like every dot on the I had to be dotted and every T had to be crossed. He never stopped walking. He was always with a purpose in mind. As the apostles were behind him they saw 1000's of pigs all over this region. And on the top of the hill was a cemetery. As Jesus reached the top of the hillside, he saw two men were naked and cut up all over their bodies running out of the tombs. The dialogue would go something like this: A sinister voice said Jesus, why have you come before your time? And Jesus said to them – Who are you? And they said they were the 12 leagues of demons. And they said to Jesus, what are you going to do with us, Jesus Son of God, for you have come before your time. Then they said to Jesus, can we go into the pigs? As they went into the pigs you could hear the shrill cries of the pigs as they went into the sea and drowned. Then miraculously the two men changed back to themselves and hugged Jesus as the apostles covered their bodies with extra clothing. Again, we see another miracle of the mystery of the number 12 occurring. Why would God come down from the vast reaches of space to come down to save two men? That is the mystery we will have to ask him about when we go up to heaven. If we were trying to title this event in the Gadarenes, we would call it an act of random kindness by God. Over the hill, there were people running with pitchforks and weapons towards them and yelling fervently. The one man of the Gadarenes said, you will have to leave Jesus, or they will kill you and your friends. So, they use the pigs to sacrifice unto the God of Zeus. Jesus smiled and departed hence back across the lake.

## "The Woman with the Issue of Blood"

There have been no coincidences in Jesus' walk from the time that he came upon this earth until the present time. Now we are going to talk about, as Jesus was in the town of Jerusalem, he was met by a crowd of 7500 people as the crowds began to get larger and larger. This story teller would like to expand on the back story of this woman with the issue of blood. She was a Samaritan woman, very petite but not old and the scribes and authors of the bible never tell us what her true age is. This is what we do know. We know she was married to a very wealthy man and because of their customs was up in age. If our dialogue was going to start with her and eventually end up with Jesus, here is how the story would go. A young hand maiden enters her bedroom and says my lady, the doctors are here for you. The lady would respond by telling the maiden to have them come in. There were two men, both of age who walked into her room. The tall lanky olive-skinned doctor says, good morning my lady. How are we feeling today? Knowing the family physician by his first name, she says, I still have the same condition that you told me (with a gruff voice) would go away, Zebulun. He said to the lady, I have brought a specialist with me who says these herbs and potions should take care of your problem. She says to the other doctor, what is your name sir? My name is Levi and I am the keeper of the apothecary, I am the sage, I am the one who takes death and brings it back to life. She says, I will try this. As she looks at the hand maiden and says prepare my chambers for these Doctors of philosophy and science. She exits behind the curtain and they follow. About 10 minutes later she comes from behind the curtain with the two men and has her hand maiden bring them a bag of coins. She asks the question, when will I know if the potion works? As they bow, and Levi says to her, you will know in a weeks' time. Meanwhile we will do three treatments a week. Then the lady says, at the rate you are going through my money I will be broke very soon. Then they bowed and exited the door. Needless to say, the story of the woman of the issue of blood did go broke by these so-called charlatans. Then one day as she was in the market place of Jerusalem, she heard of a teacher of the law, a prophet of God and a healer. She had to meet him. For now, the woman was completely broke and the issue of blood continued. As the woman was approaching Jesus and the 12 apostles she noticed she was blocked by the crowd from reaching Jesus. She did not understand the Jewish ways of a priest or rabbi that you can't touch them. The moment you would touch them they would be defiled according to Moses Law. As the crowd is erupting in adulation and they cried out, Jesus of Nazareth heal me, touch me, make me whole, it was deafening to his ears and all the ears around. Then she bid her hand maiden to step aside and she crawled between legs after legs after legs until she reached a man that she saw with a tallit. As the 4 knots, which were the representation of the word of God hung from the tallit, one of those knots in the Hebrew tongue was called zizith. As the woman of infirmity touched the knot, this would be the dialogue from Jesus to her and everyone around. As a sense of loss came over him, he said Who touched me in a loud voice not knowing who it was? As Jesus looks to Simon and Simon puts his arm around him and says to Jesus, Lord I don't know who touched you. After all there are so many people here, as many as 7500 people to greet you. Then Jesus looks down and noticed a woman kneeling at his feet and holding on to the knot. She exuberantly says, I'm healed and jumps up and turns around as Jesus slowly turns her face towards his face. As he kisses her on the forehead he says to the woman who has the issue with blood, your faith has made you whole. Go in peace. Another miracle has come and gone. What is interesting about this miracle and the mystery of the number 12 is that Jesus said to her, your faith has made you whole. As we have noticed through all the stories that the number 12 meant faith.

## "Tabatha Lives"

So as the crowds begin to disperse as the Romans have now entered the streets to keep order for the governor of Judea. Jesus has another direction in this mystery of the number 12. He heard about his friend Simon the tanner, whose daughter, named Tabatha was dead. Jesus in all his walks of everywhere he went, stopped a lot of funerals but never went to one. This would be the dialogue with the encounter of Simon the tanner. As Jesus walked up to Simons home and put his hands on his shoulder and compassionately said, I heard of your daughter's death as they both entered the house with the apostles behind them. He heard funeral marches and dirges and began to set them out of the house. For Jesus said, this is not a day of mourning but a day my father will be glorified. He told Simon, take me to her. As he entered a back room there is a young girl that was lying on her bed in graves clothes. Jesus looked at her and spoke these words: Telle Le Cumae, which means little girl arise. At that moment color and breath came into her and Tabitha said to Jesus, I'm hungry. Jesus said to Simon, she's hungry and Simon came in and hugged her and hugged Jesus. They departed hence. The mystery of the number 12 is truly amazing. From miracles. to faith, to love, to belief and lastly a remembrance.

So many things have happened and transpired so far in Jesus' walks for 3 1/2 years. He has done everything that is necessary to show his deity. He has raised the dead with Lazarus who had been dead for four days. He healed a blind man who was the high priest in his town of Nazareth, which was the only miracle he created in Nazareth at that time. He made a lame man to walk. As Jesus was hailed the Messiah, his entrance into Jerusalem would either be a triumph or a catastrophe.

## "Footnotes"

I believe that the mystery of the number 12 will be made into a book of its own or a sermon that someone will make their own. I think if we went back into the old testament and the new testament we could find more occurrences of the number 12. Fact of Fiction?

# CHAPTER 11

# THE FEAR OF CHRIST IN THE GARDEN OF GETHSEMANE

## "The Garden of Gethsemane"

The lights of the torches were beaming bright at the end of the Passover meal as John and Peter are following Jesus to his place of peace. John says to Peter the master is growing slow these last hours. Have you noticed that? Peter says as usual he is thinking about his father who is in heaven. He will be alright. We'll sit under the fig tree and pray. As Jesus turned to Peter and John and says Peter, John go over by the tree and wait for me. Don't go to sleep, stay awake for this is the hour that I have spoken about earlier. Peter and John sat down and began to pray.

## "Jesus shows his Humanity"

The moon glistens from the rock that Jesus retreats to, called the Olive Press and Jesus falls against the rock and begins to sob. When everybody was in their slumber Jesus began to shake and he slams the rock with his frail body and he looks up to Heaven and says, Father if this cup could pass from me I would ask that you do it. As the tears trickle down his cheek he closed his eyes and took his right arm and laid it across the rock and began to sob uncontrollably and looks up to heaven and says to God with a loud voice, why have you not heard my cries? Jesus says, Father I can't do this, I can't do this. Give me help, I need help. Then his right arm again touches the rock as he bows down, and he notices John and Peter see what is happening to their master. They say, we really need to pray to God for Jesus right now. He really needs our help, as they began to pray in the far distance. Jesus, through his sweat the blood begins to come out of his pores as platelets of yellow blood and he begins to shudder.

## "Jesus Reminisces"

All the peace he received by being baptized by John the Baptist and the testing he had to go through for 40 days and 40 nights and he sees himself on a pinnacle being tempted by Satan. He sees his dreams and flashbacks of how he would play soccer with the apostles, how they saw all the signs and miracles he performed. It was an amazing time how he saw the first miracle of Canaan and God was beginning to show him how important Jesus was on this earth by flashbacks of light. As lightning flashes across the sky and a loud thunderclap followed, the people heard God say, this is my Son, in whom I am well pleased. The Holy Spirit descends on his shoulder in the form of a dove. He remembers his mother as he was sitting at the marriage of Canaan and when his mother was tapping him on the leg and he was enjoying the wedding and seeing everybody in their festivities and doing the Horrah. Mary says, Jesus the man needs more wine. He looks at her with a sheepish grin and puts a grape in his mouth and says what does that have to do with me? And Jesus looks up to Heaven and realizes God wants the first miracle performed. He was reminiscing about the time the water was turned to wine, but it wasn't wine, it was the Holy Ghost. The brides' father said that that was the best wine they had ever had. He remembers the sheep as he was walking down the edges and he would carry his staff and he would see the sheep. He would tell the apostles, look see what happened? One of the sheep has put himself in the crevice. He would take the crook of the staff and reach down into the crevice and hook the baby lamb and bring it back up. He would then take the lamb and break its' legs and put it on his shoulders and carry it. He said see all these sheep here, they were lost and now they are found. He remembers and starts to smile at everything and starts to realize all the miracles that came about. He remembers the miracle of the woman of infirmity, the miracle of Tabatha, the miracle of the gathering of people, that he went about doing good and healing all those that were oppressed by the Devil. He sees everything that is happening, but he still shudders, and he is still bleeding platelets of blood. Then he turns himself and looks over and they are still praying, and he turns back around and begins to pray in his shuddered condition and in his fearful condition of going to the cross as he sees himself being flogged and as he sees himself having his beard pulled out and how they put a crown of thorns and thistle on his head. Then he looks and sees something happening.

## "Jesus Ministered by Angels"

There is a light, a brightness. He sees in a tomb, his best friend Lazarus. He says, Lazarus come forth, Lazarus come forth. I am the resurrection and the life he says. I am the resurrection and the life he says to himself. Though you were dead, now you live. He saw his friend come out of the tomb after being dead for four days and he remembered what happened with Mary of Bethany as she anointed his head for burial but actually she was anointing his head for a ceremony that would come. He knew that God the Father and him had already discussed this as El Elyon up in Heaven. The heading Jesus ministered to by angels. Jesus was lying on the ground as his head was tucked into his body almost like a fetal position. Almost like as if he was coming out of his mothers' womb and sobbing unbearably as he would raise his hands to heaven. Then Jesus said to his Father, help me, help me. You have been there with me. You have always given me what I needed. Now I ask you to help me, help me, help me. Help me get through this, to have the strength and courage, the ability to be able to go as a sacrifice for these people, these humans that you created. Help me. He got on his knees and began to pray and then suddenly, a dash of light shone bright from above and a voice from heaven came out and said, Jesus my Son, I have heard your cries. You are no different than any human being, no God trapped in a human being has gone through what you have attempted to go through. I have sent you down these angels, Raphael, Gabriel and Michael. They are going to minister to you. They have brought your favorite foods to eat and drink. So, in this last day of this last hour and these last minutes my son, go and be the sacrificial lamb. You will endure my son everything. Believe me, you will endure everything even to the cross. You will endure it as I will be with you. I will always be with you. I will never leave you or forsake you. I will be with you. As Jesus looks on and sees the angels ascending from heaven and Jesus says to them, my friends, again we meet as he hugs Gabriel, Raphael and Michael as they all begin to sit around the stone and eat the grapes and the different liquids that Jesus loved the most. Then when Jesus got his composure, Jesus says to them my friends it won't be long before I come back. Tell them, prepare them for my return and I will see you very soon. As he looks up to heaven and he says to his father as he is drenched in sweat and blood, I will accept this cup. As Jesus looks up the angels disappear into the night. He gets up off his knees and heads towards Peter and John and says to them as he shrugs their shoulders together, if you had stayed awake like I told you, you would have seen the angels minister to me. Why could you not have stayed awake for 1 hour? With a subtle look on his face he says to them, my hour has come to be turned over to the sinners.

## "Jesus is Arrested by Malak"

As Jesus is standing next to Peter and John they are approached by a crowd making a loud ruckus. The captain of the guard named Malak says to Jesus, I'm looking for Jesus. Jesus looks directly at him and says I am he that you are looking for. As one of the apostles approaches Jesus with a torch in his hand and with a kiss on his right cheek, Jesus glares into his eyes and says, so Judas now you betray me with a kiss. As the guards are about to subdue Jesus a ruckus unfolds between Peter and John as Peter removes his sword out of his scabbard and with no regards to life his sword swoops down and cuts off the ear of Malak. As he is about to impale Malak, Jesus grabs his arm and lowers it and with Jesus' steel blue eyes glaring at Peter, he says in a soft voice, if you live by the sword, you will die by the sword. Jesus softly touches Malak's ear and the ear appears where it had been severed. Malak says, he is truly the Messiah, the Christ, the Son of the Living God. Then he takes them all to the side and whispers to them, but we can not tell what we have seen this hour. For if the Sanhedrin would ever get wind of what occurred tonight we would surely be put to death. So, we will make a pact that we will never mention what happened tonight. Agreed? They all bobbed their heads in affirmation. Then Malak told Judas angrily, you got what you wanted, now leave. You will get your money from the high priest. Then Judas scurries away. Then he told the guards, take hold of Jesus and hold him fast but not too fast. He then looked at Peter and John and told them to leave before they arrest them too. As they began to yell as they held fast to Jesus and took him for his first trial.

## Footnote

As we showed in this chapter that there was a sensitive side of Jesus Christ, we saw that Jesus Christ did not want to go to the cross. As his best friends were praying for him and eventually like Christians today fall asleep, Jesus showed us how he let his beginnings show us his future. He showed us that his Father would never leave him or forsake him. He showed us that trust is everything. And most importantly he showed us his last miracle before he went to the cross. You think about it. You decide. Is it fact or fiction?

# CHAPTER 12

# THE SIX TRIALS OF CHRIST

Jesus had six trials: three religious (Jewish) and three civil (Romans). Here are the results:

First religious trial (Jewish): Ananias, John18:12–14.
Decision: Go signal given to liquidate Jesus.

Second religious trial: Caiaphas, Matthew 26:57–68.
Decision: Death sentence, charge of blasphemy, because Jesus proclaimed himself the Messiah, God the Son.

Third religious trial: Sanhedrin, Matthew 27:1–2, Luke 22:63–71
Decision: Death sentence made legal.

First civil trial (Roman): Pilate, John 18:28–38
Decision: Not guilty.

Second civil trial: Herod, Luke 23:6–12
Decision: Not guilty.

Third civil trial: Pilate again. John 18:39–19:6
Decision: Not guilty, but turned to the Jews to be crucified (Matthew 27:26).

## "The First Trial (The Removal of the Office)"

### "First Trial: Trial of Jesus in Ananias' House"

Tenth hour of the Passion: On Wednesday, from two to three o'clock in the morning. Jesus was brought bound from Gethsemane to Jerusalem, and they took him first to Ananias. Ananias was the father-in-law of Caiaphas, who was the high priest that year (John 18:12–13). Ananias had been deposed as high priest by the Romans (15 AD) and had been succeeded by Caiaphas, but Ananias still wielded great influence among the priestly families. The legal religious trial had to be done in front of the Sanhedrin, but probably there were some members of the Sanhedrin in Ananas's house, and they gave the go-ahead signal to liquidate Jesus.

You are being treated like a criminal, my sweet Jesus, I adore and praise you. I believe in you. Give me patience to accept the will of God no matter how hard it may look. Your trials, though humiliating, were to praise the Lord. Thank you, my Jesus, the only eternal one, the only one God, with the Father and the Holy Spirit. Amen.

Everything that was transpiring was in the plan of the will of God. That would later on be revealed by the historians like Josephus's. Jesus had to go before the tribune to be guilty so that he could once and for all reveal to people that he served on three and one half years of His ministry as he walked the cobbled stones and spoke in the temple and in the streets.

### "The Mouthpiece of God"

The same mouth that spoke the word into existence and banished Satan from the Garden of Eden would be the same mouthpiece that would seal his fate with the High Priest Ananias. The same mouth that said to Tabatha, the woman of infirmity for twelve years, the man of the Gadarenes, and last but not least the mouth that said "Lazarus, come forth" would hail to the whole world his deity as the son of the Godhead. Although Jesus would start to see his reign and ascension begin. He would speak the final words to the mortal beings that would make Caisphas break the priestly bind that makes him the former high priest on this earth. The transferring of power would now begin.

### "Second Trial: The Accuser of the Brethren, Denial, and the Curse is Broken"

### "Jesus in the Palace of Caiaphas"

Jesus was taken, bound, from Ananias to the palace of Caiaphas, the high priest (John 18:24). Here, the teachers of the law and the

Jewish authorities were assembled (Matthew 27:57). However, the seventy-one members of the council of the Sanhedrin could not legally hold a session during the night, so they had to have a little patience until the morning for the legal religious formal trial.

At the palace of Caiaphas, they needed some evidence against Jesus to put him to death. However, they were unable to find any. Even false witnesses came forward. Finally, "the High Priest said to Jesus: 'In the name of the living God, I command you to tell us: Are you the Messiah, the Son of God?' Then Jesus answered: 'I am, and you will see the Son of Man seated at the right hand of the Most Powerful and coming with the clouds of heaven.' At that the high Priest tore his garments and said: 'Why do we still need witnesses?' You have heard his blasphemy. What is your decision? And they all condemned Jesus saying, 'He must die' (Matthew 27:59–66; Mark 14:61–64).

Jesus was condemned to death because he claimed to be the Messiah, the Son of God, God the Son, God. The priests were not mistaken in their understanding of what Jesus claimed to be as the Son of God.

They condemned him, not because he used a blasphemous word but because in all his way of acting, Jesus put himself in a place fitting only to God. They forgot that actually they hated Jesus because he had denounced their hypocrisy, their lack of faith, and their love of money. With the sentence, they could sooth their conscience, for they, again with hypocrisy, were upholding the honor of the only one.

The title of "Messiah" has been given explicitly to Jesus only at Caesarea Philippi by Peter (Matthew 16:16; Mark 8:29), that of the Son of God only by the evil spirits and also by Peter. And in each occasion, Jesus has forbidden its public proclamation. Jesus is again called Christ (Messiah) at the cross in Mark 15:32 and Son of God also at Calvary by the centurion (Mark 15:39).

## "Jesus and the Injustice"

Jesus was condemned in the name of God. He did not rebel against the unjust sentence imposed by the religious leaders of his people who were the legal, though unworthy, representatives of God. This was his perfect obedience to the Father. I adore you, Jesus, my God. I praise you for your obedience and patience and humility, the first fruits of love. Thank you, my sweet Jesus, for so much love, for teaching me the will of the Father. Thank you, my friend Jesus.

## "The Denials of Peter"

Peter denied Jesus three times at the courtyard of the palace of Caiaphas. "He denied Him with an oath, swearing, 'I do not know that man' . . . and the third time, 'Peter begun justifying himself with curses and oaths protesting that he did not know the man Jesus . . . and just then a cock crowed. And Peter remembered the words of Jesus, 'Before the cock crows, you will deny me three times. And he went away weeping bitterly'" (Matthew 26:58, 69–75).

Luke adds, "The Lord turned around and looked at Peter . . . Peter went outside, weeping bitterly" (Luke 22:61). You can bet this "look" of Jesus to Peter was with all his love, the dearest "look" in the history of mankind, only comparable to the several ones Jesus gave to Judas.

We already commented on the sins and the difference of Peter and Judas.

All the disciples already had abandoned Jesus at Gethsemane. They all deserted him and fled (Mark 14:50), including Peter and John, all. However, Peter and John followed Jesus at a distance (John 22:54; John 18:15). Judas has already been the "traitor." And now Peter denies Jesus under oath and curses. My lovely, sweet Jesus, I love you. I thank you for so much love and so much patience and so much humility. Yes, you are God, the only God, with the Holy Spirit, in the glory of God the Father, and the Father is like you. Because he who sees you sees the Father (John 14:9). Yes, my Jesus, the Father is like you: loving and patient, and humble. I praise you, Lord, thank you, my friend Jesus.

The apostles did not lack character or courage; if so, Jesus would not have chosen them. Peter was sincere when he said, "Although all abandon you, I will not." They were all ready to die for Jesus. But when Jesus was arrested, the apostles became confused because he did not use his divine power and showed no resistance to his enemies. It would be wrong to say that the apostles were cowards until they received the Holy Spirit. Their reaction is understandable. However, their fleeing shook to the foundation all the faith they had after living day by day with Jesus for the past three years, a faith fully restored at Pentecost with superabundance.

It was not fear that caused Peter to deny Jesus: it was human weakness, just in front of servant maids. We are all weak. The denial of Peter was real and a most serious fall, but God forgives the sin the instant Peter's gaze meets Jesus, and Peter repents and trusts in Jesus (Luke 22:61). The failure, however, will compel Peter to the end of his life, not to rely on himself but on the Lord. Peter Rock, which is the same word in Hebrew, became the head of the church of Jesus. That's how God forgives and forgets. Please look at chapter 10. But he would remain ever conscious of his personal weakness and never find peace until he followed Jesus by dying on a cross with the head down, giving up his life for Jesus. Praise the Lord (John 21:19).

## "Mockery of Jesus by the Soldiers and Jesus in Prison"

Eleventh Hour of the Passion: Wednesday from three to four o'clock in the morning

Immediately after the condemnation, "some of them begun to spit on Jesus and, blindfolding him, they struck him saying, 'Play the Prophet!' Who hit you? Who spit on you? And the guard set upon him with blows" (Mark 15:65).

They played the "game of the king" of the Jews, and Jesus was the center of all the mockery. Today, in Jerusalem, in the Church of the Sisters of Zion, there is the lithostratos with the floor marked with some of the games the Roman soldiers used to play. One of these can be identified by the letter B, which stands for the Greek word basileus (king) or "the game of the king." One of the few places where Jesus actually walked.

I love you, Jesus, God. God. God. Heavens and earth are full of your glory. Hosanna in the highest. Blessed are you, Jesus, who comes in the name of the Lord. Thank you, my friend Jesus. I am the one who spits on your face when I sin and the one who hits you. Have mercy of me and of the whole world. Thank you, my dear friend Jesus (Hebrews 6:6).

At that hour, there was a trumpet being blown in Zion, for the return of the king to his rightful place was about to begin, as the high priest of the office in that day and hour had given up his right to have such an office. Like the passing of a baton from one kingship to the other or like the games where a runner who is in a race gives over to a stronger and more viral runner with more stamina in his bones and sinew.

### "Jesus Before Caiaphas Again and the Sanhedrin"

Twelfth Hour of the Passion: Wednesday from four to five o'clock in the morning.

The Sanhedrin was the one to give the religious sentence to Jesus, but it was illegal for the seventy-one members of the Sanhedrin to meet at night. So Jesus had to wait until the morning, and it is the time the soldiers used to mock Jesus. And when they were tired of the game, they put him in a kind of prison, where he had to be brought from the only entrance, a hole on the top. And the room is so small that the body could fit only standing; it could not bend. I saw this kind of prison in Jerusalem, I believe near the Galli-Canto area.

Then "very early in the morning, the chief priests, the elders and the teachers of the Law, that is, the whole Council of Sanhedrin, had their plan ready. They put Jesus in chains, led him away and handed him to Pilate" (Mark 15:1; Matthew 27:1; Luke 22:66–23:1).

## "The Chains of Our Afflictions He Bore"

I love you, Jesus in chains. I adore you, and I believe and trust in you. I am the one who put you in chains whenever I sin. Have mercy of me and of the whole world. Thank you, my dear friend Jesus.

The chains became the symbol of a statement that Jesus made. In Matthew 16:19, we read as follows:

"And I will give unto thee [Peter] the keys of the kingdom of heaven: and whatsoever thou shalt bind on earth shall be bound in heaven: and whatsoever thou shalt loose on earth shall be loosed in heaven."

This saying seems to be patterned on Isaiah 22:22 (I shall quote verses 20–23 for context):

"And it shall come to pass in that day, that I will call my servant Eliakim the son of Hilkiah:

"And I will clothe him with thy robe, and strengthen him with thy girdle, and I will commit thy government into his hand: and he shall be a father to the inhabitants of Jerusalem, and to the house of Judah.

"And the key of the house of David will I lay upon his shoulder; so he shall open, and none shall shut; and he shall shut, and none shall open."

Here, my father wrote in his Greek notes {link to his notes}:

The Greek really reads "whatsoever thou shalt bind on earth shall have been already bound in heaven: and whatsoever thou shalt loose on earth shall have been already loosed in heaven." Quite the opposite meaning from the King James Version. With this King James Version reading, Christians control what heaven will do. But heaven controls the Christian.

## "Fourth Trial Was Before Pontius Pilate"

The law is no longer the Talmud. The law is now the Roman Code of Criminal Procedure. And there were four steps that they must follow to make this an accurate court of law. We'll carry them through one by one.

First, here's a little background on Pilate. He was an anti-Semitic Spain-born Gentile. He was appointed by Caesar to govern Judea. He is what we would call the governor of the state, though in those days, they had provinces. Pilate was a marked man in the mind of Caesar and also his court, because of the number of revolutions that had broken out under his rule. He had made some unwise decisions. He had murdered some Jews. He had tightened the screws of Roman requirements. He lacked diplomacy. Therefore, the state over which he served was in turmoil.

Caesar, with tactic approval, left him there as governor, but he was under investigation at this particular time. After the trial and death of Jesus, Pilate was banished to Gall, and while he was there, he died of suicide. Pilate was a very unstable man, and because of a few political maneuverings on his part, he became the governor of a province.

The time was around six thirty to seven o'clock in the morning.

John 18:28: "Then led they Jesus from Caiaphas unto the hall of judgment: and it was early; and they themselves went not into the judgment hall, lest they should be defiled; but that they might eat the Passover."

They were criminal in attitude, but they were extremely legal in their religion. The Talmud stated that no Jew could enter a Gentile court on Passover, or he would be defiled. So they stayed out of the court itself, and apparently, Pilate came out to them.

John 18:29: "Pilate then went out unto them."

You'll see him coming out and going back in continuous fashion. Now, the first law of Roman criminal code in its procedure was accusation. That's the first thing that Pilate covered.

John 18:29–30: "What accusation bring ye against this man? They answered and said unto him, 'If he were not a malefactor, we would not have delivered him up unto thee.'"

This is a sarcastic answer and did not answer Pilate's question. "If he was not guilty, we wouldn't be here, Pilate!"

John 18:31: "Then said Pilate unto them, Take ye him, and judge him according to your law."

Pilate doesn't know that it's a capital punishment under way. He simply said, "If it's a problem in your law, then you take him, and you judge him."

John 18:31: "The Jews therefore said unto him, 'It is not lawful for us to put any man to death.'"

This changes the whole thing. From the other Gospels, they declared that he's guilty of treason and that he claimed to be another Caesar.

John 18:33: "Then Pilate entered into the judgment hall again."

You see, he's entering in again. John 18:33: "And called Jesus."

The second law of Roman criminal code in its procedure, after accusation, was interrogation, to probe and search for evidence against the man. Thus, the following questions:

John 18:33–35: "Art thou the King of the Jews? Jesus answered him, 'Sayest thou this thing of thyself, or did others tell it thee of me?' Pilate answered, 'Am I a Jew? Thine own nation and the chief priests have delivered thee unto me: what hast thou done?'"

He wanted to know if Jesus was in the process of overthrowing the government in Palestine.

John 18:36: "Jesus answered, 'My kingdom is not of this world: if my kingdom were of this world, then would my servants fight, that I should not be delivered to the Jews: but now is my kingdom not from hence.'"

If Jesus wanted to overthrow the government, his servants would be fighting, carrying on a revolution, taking lives, storming this temple, and ruining this procedure. "But you don't even find my servants out there."

The third process in the Roman code was defense. And now Pilate, acting on behalf of a defense attorney, began to look at this side of Jesus. By the way, the Roman law, much like

American law, allowed for a defense attorney, but you never find where Jesus was allowed that. So Pilate looks at it from Jesus's point of view. "So you're a king!"

John 18:37: "Pilate therefore said unto him, 'Art thou a king then?' Jesus answered, 'Thou sayest that I am a king. To this end was I born, and for this cause came I into the world, that I should bear witness unto the truth. Everyone that is of the truth heareth my voice.'"

John 18:38: "Pilate saith unto him, 'What is truth?'"

This has nothing to do with the case. It has a lot to do with Pilate's mindset. He was a very mixed-up, miserable man. In a matter of months, he would be taking his own life. He is in a quandary regarding the area of objective, sound truth. And so he says, "What's truth?"

John 18:38: "And when he had said this, he went out again unto the Jews, and saith unto them, I find in him no fault at all."

The fourth step is a verdict. Accusation, interrogation, defense, and a verdict. And all four are acted out for us right here. Pilate says he finds no guilt. All he finds is some spiritual kingdom, and that's not going to affect or threaten Rome. Jesus is not guilty of treason.

Luke 23:4–5: "Then said Pilate to the chief priests and to the people, I find no fault in this man. And they were the more fierce, saying, He stirreth up the people, teaching throughout all Judea, beginning from Galilee to this place."

As Herod spoke to the Chief Priest Ciaphas, so this is the Jesus that I heard about who turned water into wine. Ciaphas said, I don't know, I have not heard of such a thing. Jesus spoke and said, yes it is true. Then before my court Jesus and the Chief Priest as he pours the water into the goblet and raises it over his head and he says to Jesus, if you turn this water into wine I will free you. As murmuring occurred all over the kings halls, Silence he says. You dare question your king? Jesus of Nazareth turn this water into wine. As Jesus closes his eyes and begins to pray for the water to be turned to wine, then Herod with his irrational behavior starts to drink from the goblet. He then turns to Jesus and says why has thou not turned this water into wine as I commanded thee? Jesus says, I did what asked for, what I have given you is from my father in heaven, which is the best wine that you will ever have. As he finishes the goblet he becomes very giddy and backs into his throne. It is as if he is in a drunken stupor. He calls to the Captain of the guards and says, place my purple robe around him. I find no fault in him. Take him back to Pilate.

Now when Pilate heard the word "Galilee," he had an ingenious idea. Galilee really wasn't his jurisdiction, and since he didn't want this case, he tried to find somebody else to try Jesus.

## "Fifth Trial Before Herod, the King of the Jews"

Luke 23:6–7: "When Pilate heard of Galilee, he asked whether the man were a Galilean. And as soon as he knew that he belonged unto Herod's jurisdiction, he sent him to Herod, who himself also was at Jerusalem at that time."

Herod was his lifelong enemy up until this event. Herod's the one who beheaded John the Baptist. He's the one who dealt with vicious cruelty over his subjects. Now, Herod has looked upon Jesus as a magician, and he has been excited to see Jesus do a trick.

Luke 23:8: "And when Herod saw Jesus, he was exceeding glad: for he was desirous to see him of a long season, because he had heard many things of him; and he hoped to have seen some miracle done by him."

By the way, you do not see where Jesus responds to Herod in any way. It was no proceeding at all. All Herod wanted was a game. He wanted a jester for his court. He wanted a clown. When Jesus wouldn't cooperate, we read that they mocked him as a king.

Luke 23:10–11: "And the chief priests and scribes stood and vehemently accused him. And Herod with his men of war set him at nought, and mocked him, and arrayed him in a gorgeous robe, and sent him again to Pilate."

## "Sixth Trial Back to Pilate"

Now back at the palace, Pilate was probably eating breakfast and thinking, Whew! That's over. And he looks out his window, and there came Jesus back, bound and robed as a king. It was obvious to Pilate that Herod was not in any cooperative mood. The whole event brought Herod and Pilate together as friends.

Luke 23:12: "And the same day Pilate and Herod were made friends together: for before they were at enmity between themselves."

Pilate did not want to declare him guilty, so he tried several avenues to get out of that verdict. The first thing he offered was to chastise and beat Jesus, then release him, but they said no. The second thing he tried to do was release Jesus through a custom they had. It was a custom to release a prisoner on the Passover.

Matthew 27:15: "Now at that feast the governor was wont to release unto the people a prisoner, whom they would."

Barabbas was a notorious criminal. He was a murderer. He was an insurrectionist. He was guilty of sedition, and he was bound in prison awaiting death by crucifixion. It was a capital crime he had committed. He was the one guilty of treason. So Pilate thought that if he were to put Barabbas next to Jesus and offered to release one of them, the crowd would say, "Don't release Barabbas! Release Jesus!" But it backfired upon him. They said they wanted Jesus crucified (Matthew 27:19–23).

Pilate says to the crowd as he extends his hands to Jesus, it is the custom of Rome to release, as he bellows out to the crowd one prisoner at the time of Passover. He then again extends his arms to Jesus and then says, do I release Jesus of Nazareth or Barabbas?

The crowd begins to yell as they begin the sixth trial. Who would think that just a few days earlier this same crowd would be cheering on Jesus in his triumphant entry into Jerusalem. Now they are asking to release Barabbas and put this frail, worn down body to be crucified as they utter in agreement. Give us Barabbas, give us Barabbas as his followers begin chanting.

Then what do we do with this man Jesus, Pontius Pilate asked? The people and the followers of Barabbas army say to Pontius Pilate, crucify him, crucify him, crucify him not knowing that the 6th trial of Christ was being held by the people themselves. Pontius Pilate then summons one of his guards to bring him a bowl of water with a cloth. He then says to the crowd as he places his hands in the water, then wipes his hands with the cloth, I wash my hands of this innocent man. He then looks at the two guards holding Jesus and says to them, do what they say. He then turns to the temple and resumes his duty.

So then they gathered a whole band of soldiers, stripped him, put him in a scarlet robe, placed a crown of thorns on his head and a reed in his right hand, and mocked him by bowing down and saying, "Hail, king of the Jews!" And they struck him on the head, spit upon him, and led him away to be crucified (Matthew 27:26–31).

**"Footnotes"**

You and I deserve that spit. We deserve the nails in his feet and hands. It's our sin he bore, not his. It's our place he took, not the Father's. We are the guilty ones. We are like sheep gone astray, turned everyone to our own ways. We are the rebels. Our iniquity has separated us from God, not his. But the message in all of this is because of love. He did it for us. He became sin for us.

Here is a true and intriguing story of someone's experience. A minister of God didn't have anyone to work with, so he asked God to make him available to whatever would be His will. He checked the want ads because he needed some money, and he saw there was a bus-driving job made available to him. So he worked as a bus driver in South Chicago. If you know anything about Chicago, it's not South Chicago you want to drive a bus in, but that's where they had the need. He found out later it was because nobody else would stay on the job. So he drove it.

Before a week passed, some thugs got on the bus and didn't pay. They sat in the back, sneered, jeered, and mocked him. The next day, the same thing happened. The third day, it happened again. After it went on for about a week, he decided he didn't have to put up with that. So he decided to call an officer inside the bus and make them pay. He saw one down about a block, and after he got on, he told the officer that the fellows back there haven't paid for several days. Would you at least make them pay today? And he did, but unfortunately, the officer got off the bus. When the door was closed, the bus driver drove a little farther and turned a corner, and that was the last thing he remembered. They knocked a couple of teeth out of his head. They stole his money, and when he woke up, the bus was empty.

He sat there in confusion and disillusionment, wondering, What kind of ministry is this, Lord? I told you I was available and this was the job you opened up? And he went home, turned the bus in, and took the rest of the day off. He stared up at the ceiling as he was nursing his wounds, and he thought, I'm not gonna let them get away with that. So through an interesting chain of events, they rounded up, with the help of some officers, the very fellows and took them to court. All four of them.

On the day of the hearing he stood before the court, and the judge listened carefully and decided the fellows were guilty. And they didn't have any money to buy their way out, so they had to spend some time in jail. Suddenly, the minister realized, Here's my chance. He said, "Your honor, may I speak for a few moments." The judge said, "Yes, you may." The minister said, "I'd like for you to tally up all of the time these fellows together would be spending in jail, and I'd like to go in their behalf." And the judge responded, "Well, that's highly irregular. It has never been done before." And the minister responded, "Oh yes, it has. About two thousand years ago." And then in about four minutes, he gave them the Gospel.

Three of the young men came to know Christ on the spot. One of them later, after the minister was incarcerated. That fellow was having a ministry with those four guys who heard the message that somebody else wanted to pay the price for their sin. A living testimony for what Jesus did for us.

Fact or Fiction. You decide.

CHAPTER **13**

# THE GARDEN OF EDEN VS THE CURSE IS BROKEN

"It is finished"

There are so many interpretations to the cross and the symbol that it stands for in modern-day religion. Some say it was a way for man's sins to be washed away. Though some have come to another scenario just like myself that it was a way to start from the beginning. You see, if sin originated at the Garden of Eden, then why do so many people try to depict it at the cross what really happened? Jesus always tried to talk in parables. But one common denominator was that Adam sinned, and he was the second Adam.

## "God Is Always Cleaning Up Our Messes"

He was going to do whatever he had to do to put back in place what man seems to all mess up. Everyone knows what I am talking about. We get the good things in life from God, and then we turn around and just make a fool and a shamble of our lives. I don't know how many times from a personal standpoint that I didn't listen to God and turned around and found myself busted and disgusted. That is not a place where God wants us to be. Why is it that we always do our way wrong and God always does it right?

## "Taking My Eyes Off the Prize"

I was listening to a person the other day telling me that they have to be wealthy because they want everything, and will do whatever it takes to get it done. I started to research that, and I realized that Adam and Eve also took their eyes off the prize. Now the serpent was more subtle than any beast of the field that the Lord God had made. And he said unto the woman, "Yea, hath God said, Ye shall not eat of every tree of the garden?"

## "Back to the Garden of Eden"

Isn't it amazing that God had to go back to the beginning of sin, at the Garden of Eden? That is where the first Adam gave up his dominion for a piece of fruit.

## "The First Blame Shift"

Many historians have tried to blame everything on the woman and that she made him do it. God has certain guidelines that he puts down anytime that he puts someone in charge. Adam was the caretaker of His garden. He saw the serpent coming into the garden, and he could have eradicated him but chose to allow it, like Christians today do the same thing. They need to go to the cross to get rid of their sin. Make sure though when you do go to the tree of good and evil, do not eat the fruit, for when you eat of it you will surely die" (New International Version, Genesis 2:15–17).

## "The Tree of Knowledge of Life and Death"

A confirmation of his present happiness to him, in that grant, "Of every tree in the garden thou mayest freely eat." This was not only an allowance of liberty to him, in taking the delicious fruits of paradise, as a recompense for his care and pains in dressing and keeping it (1 Corinthians 9:7, 10). But it was, withal, an assurance of life to him, immortal life, upon his obedience. For the tree of life being put in the midst of the garden (Genesis 2:9), as the heart and soul of it, doubtless, God had an eye to that especially in this grant. And therefore, when, upon his revolt, this grant is recalled, no notice is taken of any tree of the garden as prohibited to him, except the tree of life (Genesis 3:22), of which it is said he might have eaten and lived forever, that is, never died nor ever lost his happiness. "Continue holy as thou art, in conformity to thy Creator's will, and thou shalt continue happy as thou art in the enjoyment of thy Creator's favour, either in this paradise or in a better." Thus, upon condition of perfect personal and perpetual obedience, Adam was sure of paradise to himself and his heirs forever.

## "The Trial of Obedience Was Shattered"

A trial of his obedience, upon pain of the forfeiture of all his happiness: "But of the other tree which stood very near the tree of life (for they are both said to be in the midst of the garden), and which was called the tree of knowledge, in the day thou eatest thereof, thou shalt surely die," as if he had said, "Know, Adam, that thou art now upon thy good behaviour, thou art put into paradise upon trial; be observant, be obedient, and thou art made for ever; otherwise thou wilt be as miserable as now thou art happy." Here, (1.) Adam is threatened with death in case of disobedience: Dying thou shalt die, denoting a sure and dreadful sentence, as, in the former part of this covenant, eating thou shalt eat denotes a free and full grant. Observe [1.] Even Adam, innocence, was awed with a threatening; fear is one of the handles of the soul, by which it is taken hold of and held. If he then needed this hedge, much more do we now. [2.] The penalty threatened is death: Thou shalt die, that is, "Thou shalt be debarred from the tree of life, and all the good that is signified by it, all the happiness thou hast, either in possession or prospect; and thou shalt become liable to death, and all the miseries that preface it and attend it." [3.] This was threatened as the immediate consequence of sin: In the day thou eatest, thou shalt die, that is, "Thou shalt become mortal and capable of dying; the grant of immortality shall be recalled, and that defence shall depart from thee. Thou shalt become obnoxious to death, like a condemned malefactor that is dead in the law" (only because Adam was to be the root of mankind, he was reprieved); "nay, the harbingers and forerunners of death shall immediately seize thee, and thy life, thenceforward, shall be a dying life: and this, surely; it is a settled rule, the soul that sinneth, it shall die."

Adam is tried with a positive law not to eat of the fruit of the tree of knowledge. Now it was very proper to make trial of his obedience by such a command as this. [1.] Because the reason of it is fetched purely from the will of the law maker. Adam had in his nature an aversion to that which was evil in itself, and therefore, he is tried in a thing that was evil only because it was forbidden. And being in a small thing, it was the more fit to prove his obedience by. [2.] Because the restraint of it is laid upon the desires of the flesh and of the mind that, in the corrupt nature of man, are the two great fountains of sin. This prohibition checked both his appetite toward sensitive delights and his ambitions of curious knowledge, that his body might be ruled by his soul and his soul by his God.

Thus easy, thus happy, was man in a state of innocence, having all that heart could wish to make him so. How good was God to him? How many favors did he lead him with? How easy were the laws he gave him? How kind the covenant he made with him? Yet man, being in honor, understood not his own interest but soon became as the beasts that perish.

## "No Place to Hide"

A lot of times, we have no place to hide, as we try to get away from God's love for us. Some of us just give up and give in to what the devil wants us to do. We go back to the murk and the mire, and then he has us there, right where he wants us. The Hebrew children did the same thing in Egypt as well. They wanted someone else to take care of them, and that is why they didn't hear from the I Am because of their stiff-neck attitude. They were forced to roam through unsheltered desert until one by one they died off. They died off with no reservation of why they had no place to hide. Where the road that we choose sometimes becomes very bumpy with many pitfalls. We belly ache and cry, and then we walk off the path unaware of the outcome to unchartered regions.

## "Jesus Is the Answer"

If we want to get set free of the fiery darts of the devil, then we have to remember the facts about the Garden of Eden. The factual data of the Garden of Eden is that they both fell from grace at that time. Jesus had to be the sacrificial lamb that brings everything back into focus. Jesus is the godly glue that holds the universe together. Jesus saw the opportunity to restore the first Adam and reconcile him back to the Father.

## "The Curse of the First Adam"

"And I will put enmity between thee and the woman, and between thy seed and her seed; it shall bruise thy head, and thou shalt bruise his heel" (Genesis 3:15). In order to understand God's viewpoint, we have to understand that everything has to be in order and not in chaos. God will reconcile everything back to himself, but there is reciprocity that we must face for our actions. We see that enmity was first the decision set forth by the maker to separate them from him. God is pure, and He is Holy. And since the audible voice was Jesus's, He couldn't even look upon sin. There was an apostasy that made Adam and Eve an enemy of God. Yet God in all his love for them, who could have destroyed them? He did want any father would do when his child was in disobedience. Every Father who loves their child will punish their child the way he sees fit to do it. The dialogue would go something like this: Unto Adam he said, "Because thou hast hearkened unto the voice of thy wife, and hast eaten of the tree, of which I commanded thee, saying, Thou shalt not eat of it: cursed [is] the ground for thy sake; in sorrow shalt thou eat [of] it all the days of thy life" (Genesis 3:18–21). "Thorns also and thistles shall it bring forth to thee; and thou shalt eat the herb of the field; In the sweat of thy face shalt thou eat bread, till thou return unto the ground; for out of it wast thou taken: for dust thou [art], and unto dust shalt thou return. And Adam called his wife's name Eve; because she was the mother of all living. Unto Adam also and to his wife did the LORD God make coats of skins, and clothed them."

## "Jesus Restores and Breaks the Curse"

To make us to be able to understand God would mean to understand the meaning of life. You see, Jesus was the plan from the beginning. Who else would be able to reconcile himself back to himself than God? When the thorns and thistles were placed around the Garden of Eden, no one could ever enter into the hallowed grounds until God gave permission to let it happen. Even to this day, there are archeologists that have said when looking for the Garden of Eden, they seem to almost lose their engine as they sputter and spurt. They get near the Tigress and the Euphrates, and something seems to always keep them at bay. I believe that it is because of the sword of the Angel of the Lord that is preventing man from entering into the utopia. Therefore, the Lord God sent him forth from the Garden of Eden to till the ground from whence he was taken (Genesis 3:24). So he drove out the man, and he placed at the east of the Garden of Eden cherubims and a flaming sword that turned every way to keep the way of the tree of life.

## "Why the Crown of Thorns and Thistle?"

Do you know that Jesus could have had a crown of any magnitude put on his head? No one who was up for insurrection against the state was ever given such honors. Yet, why was a crown of thorns put on his head? I believe that the answer takes us back to the Garden of Eden. When the first Adam sinned, God made references to the serpent's heel would be bruised by the seed. The seed was the second Adam also known as Jesus Christ, the anointed one of God. I learned one important aspect in the teachings of Jesus Christ. Everything he did was in the chronological order that he chooses and not man. The reasoning he had the thorn and thistles was very evident. When the Garden of Eden was shut for good, only the blood of Jesus could eradicate sin. The evidence of the crown became apparent.

## "Blood Washes Away the Sin"

As the Roman soldiers were preparing the last high priest for his office, they twisted a crown of thorns and thistle. When the crown was placed on his head and the blood rushed to his right ear, the Garden of Eden was broken of the curse from the first Adamic era. The blood is the only thing that can wash away my sins and your sins. We think that we can do it on our own, but we really can't. It takes a savior, a sacrificial lamb to be placed at the altar of indifference in today's society. There is always a plan by the creator to make a way where there is no way. He is the way maker of yesterday, today, and forever.

## "The Parable of the Good Samaritan"

Sometimes we reach back in the recesses of our minds to understand the types and shadows of the dimensions of the Bible. A man was going down from Jerusalem to Jericho, when he fell into the hands of robbers. They stripped him of his clothes, beat him, and went away, leaving him half dead. This is really the story about not to be a good neighbor or do unto others as you would want them to do unto you. No, my friends this is a story about how the devil stripped us of our inheritance, and in this, we focus on Adam as we show him being stripped of his inheritance. Don't we call Satan a thief and a robber? The next thing that occurred was that he was left half dead. God told him that the day he ate of the tree of knowledge, he would truly die. The first person that sees this man is a priest, and the priest is afraid that he would be defiled if he touched him. Then the next person was a Levite, and he also was afraid to be defiled, and he was afraid and went around him. Then the good Samaritan, who also was a half Jew, saw that the man was in torment. Well wasn't Jesus a Samaritan since he was from a Jewish family and the Son of God? He had compassion on him, and he didn't want to see him die. That is how God is with you and me. We sometimes get so, although he is still willing to lift you out of the despair and desperation that we face in life.

## "Binding Up the Wounds by the First Sacrifice"

Then He bound up his wounds on Adam and killed the first animal for sacrifice. I wonder if we ever see God if we ask him if it was a lamb that His skin is made of. That would be interesting for reading material. Has God bound your wounds up for you? What are you doing to help your friends and neighbors and through the power of the Holy Spirit release the curse that has fallen on their lives? After all, we all have sinned and fall short of the glory of God. The only way to break the curse is to not allow it to pass on to the next generation.

## "The Curse of Today"

I believe the reason why we are having so many problems about the curse of today is because of the curse of Adam and the Garden of Eden. "This know also, that in the last days perilous times shall come" (2 Timothy 3:1). Why don't we look at the curses of Deuteronomy 28:16–62? All the curses that were brought upon the land, because of the Garden of Eden. Jesus would be the answer to remove the sin and sacrifice once and for all. Like he said, it is finished. Yet, don't forget that in today's society, people are caught up in self, apostasy in the nostrils of God. Children no longer respect their parents and only care for what they will receive and accomplish through the icons of the Power Rangers. They are made up of five characters based upon the power and driven force for parents trying to please them instead of God. They do not allow God to be their number one in finances and in love. The list of actions that Timothy was told by Paul would happen. Truly, dangerous times are upon us.

The words contain a warning of imminent dangers. And there are four things in them: First, the manner of the warning: "This know also." Second, the evil itself that they are warned of: "Perilous times." Third, the way of their introduction: "They shall come." Fourth, the time and season of it: "They shall come in the last days."

First. The manner of the warning: "This know also." "Thou Timothy, unto the other instructions which I have given thee how to behave thyself in the house of God, whereby thou mayest be set forth as a pattern unto all gospel ministers in future ages, I must also add this, 'This know also.' It belongs to thy duty and office to know and consider the impending judgments that are coming upon churches." And so as a justification of my present design, if God enable me unto it, I shall here premise that it is the duty of the ministers of the Gospel to foresee and take notice of the dangers that the churches are falling into. And the Lord help us, and all other ministers, to be awakened unto this part of our duty. You know how God sets it forth (Ezekiel 33) in the parable of the watchman to warn men of approaching dangers. And truly, God hath given us this law: If we warn the churches of their approaching dangers, we discharge our duty; if we do not, their blood will be required at our hands. The Spirit of God foresaw negligence apt to grow upon us in this matter; and therefore, the scripture only proposeth duty on the one hand and on the other requires the people's blood at the hands of the watchmen, if they perform not their duty. So speaks the prophet Isaiah, chapter 21, verse 8, "He cried, A lion: My lord, I stand continually upon the watch-tower." A lion is an emblem of approaching judgment. "The lion hath roared; who can but tremble?" saith the prophet Amos. It is the duty of ministers of the Gospel to give warning of impending dangers.

Again, the apostle, in speaking unto Timothy, speaks unto us also, to us all, "This know ye also." It is the great concern of all Christian professors and believers of all churches to have their hearts very much fixed upon present and approaching dangers. We have inquired so long about signs, tokens, and evidences of deliverance, and I know not what, that we have almost lost the benefit of all our trials, afflictions, and persecutions. The duty of all believers is to be intent upon present and imminent dangers. "O Lord," say the disciples, Matthew 24, "what shall be the sign of thy coming?" They were fixed upon His coming. Our Savior answers, "I will tell you:

There shall be an abounding of errors and false teachers: many shall say, 'Lo here is Christ,' and, 'Lo, there is Christ.'

There shall be an apostasy from holiness: 'iniquity shall abound, and the love of many shall wax cold.'

There shall be great distress of nations: 'Nation shall rise against nation, and kingdom against Kingdom.' There shall be great persecutions: 'And they shall persecute you, and bring you before rulers; and you shall be hated of all men for my name's sake.'

There shall be great tokens of God's wrath from heaven: 'Signs in the heavens, the sun, moon, and stars.'"

The Lord Christ would acquaint believers how they should look for His coming; He tells them of all the dangers. Be intent upon these things. I know you are apt to overlook them; but these are the things that you are to be intent upon.

Not to be sensible of a present perilous season is that security that the scripture so condemns; and I will leave it with you, in short, under these three things:

It is that frame of heart that, of all others, God doth most detest and abhor. Nothing is more hateful to God than a secure frame in perilous days.

I will not fear to say this, and go with it, as to my sense, to the day of judgment: A secure person, in perilous seasons, is assuredly under the power of some predominant lust, whether it appears or not.

This secure, senseless frame is the certain presage of approaching ruin. This know, brethren, pray know this, I beg of you, for yours and my own soul, that you will be sensible of, and affected with, the perils of the season where into we are cast. What they are, if God help me, and give me a little strength, I shall show you by-and-by.

Secondly. There is the evil and danger itself thus forewarned of, and that is hard times, perilous times, times of great difficulty, like those of public plagues, when death lies at every door, times that I am sure we shall not all escape. Let it fall where it will. I will say no more of it now because it is that which I shall principally speak to afterward.

Third. The manner of their introduction "shall come." We have no word in our language that will express the force of the original. The Latins express it by "immineno, incido"—the coming down of a fowl unto his prey. Now, our translators have given it the greatest force they could. They do not say, "Perilous times will come," as though they prognosticated future events;

but "perilous times shall come." Here is a hand of God in this business. They shall so come, be so instant in their coming that nothing shall keep them out. They shall instantly press themselves in and prevail. Our great wisdom then will be to eye the displeasure of God in perilous seasons since there is a judicial hand of God in them, and we see in ourselves reason enough why they should come. But when shall they come?

Fourth. They "shall come in the last days." The words "latter" or "last days" are taken three ways in scripture: sometimes for the times of the Gospel, in opposition to the Judaical church-state, as in Hebrews 1:2, "Hath in these last days spoken unto us by his Son" and elsewhere it may be taken (though I remember not the place) for days toward the consummation of all things and the end of the world. And it is taken often for the latter days of churches. 1 Timothy 4:1: "The Spirit of vile lusts, and the practice of horrible sins." This rendered the seasons perilous. Whether this be such a season or not, do you judge? And I must say, by the way, we may and ought to witness against it and mourn for the public sins of the days wherein we live. It is a glorious thing to be a martyr for bearing testimony against the public sins of an age, as in bearing testimony unto any truth of the Gospel whatsoever.

Now, where these things are, a season is perilous:

1.  Because of the infection. Churches and professors are apt to be infected with it. The historians tell us of a plague at Athens, in the second and third years of the Peloponnesian War, whereof multitudes died. And of those that lived, few escaped, but they lost a limb, or part of a limb—some an eye, others an arm, and others a finger. The infection was so great and terrible. And

truly, brethren, where this plague comes—of the visible practice of unclean lusts under an outward profession came from the Garden of Eden curse. Though men do not die, yet one loses an arm, another an eye, another a leg by it: the infection diffuses itself to the best of professors, more or less. This makes it a dangerous and perilous time.

2. It is dangerous because of the effects. For when predominant lusts have broken all bounds of divine light and rule, how long do you think that human rules will keep them in order? They break through all in such a season as the apostle describes. And if they come to break through all human restraints as they have broken through divine, they will fill all things with ruin and confusion.

3. They are perilous in the consequence, which is the judgments of God. So 2 Thessalonians 2:10–11 is a description how the papacy came upon the world. Men professed the truth of religion but did not love it. They loved unrighteousness and ungodliness, and God sent them popery. That is the interpretation of the place, according to the best divines. Will you profess the truth and at the same time love unrighteousness? The consequence is security under superstition and ungodliness. This is the end of such a perilous season, and the like may be said as to temporal judgments, which I need not mention.

Let us now consider what is our duty in such a perilous season:

We ought greatly to mourn for the public abominations of the world and of the land of our nativity wherein we live. I would only observe that place in Ezekiel 9:4. God sends out His judgments and destroys the city. But before, He sets a mark upon the foreheads of the men that sigh and cry out for all the abominations that are done in the midst thereof. You will find this passage referred to in your books as Revelation 7:3, "Hurt not the earth, neither the sea, nor the trees, till we have sealed the servants of our God in their foreheads." I would only observe this, that such only are the servants of God, let men profess what they will, "who mourn for the abominations that are done in the land." The mourners in the one place are the servants of God in the other. And truly, brethren, we are certainly to blame in this matter. We have been almost well contented that men should be as wicked as they would themselves, and we sit still and see what would come of it. Christ hath been dishonored, the Spirit of God blasphemed, and God provoked against the land of our nativity. And yet we have not been affected with these things. I can truly say in sincerity, I bless God. I have sometimes labored with my own heart about it. But I am afraid we, all of us, come exceedingly short of our duty in this matter. "Rivers of waters," saith the Psalmist, "run down mine eyes, because men keep not thy law." Horrible profanation of the name of God, horrible abominations, which our eyes have seen and our ears heard, and yet our hearts have been unaffected with them. Do you think this is a frame of heart God requireth of us in such a season—to be regardless of all and not to mourn for the public abominations of the land? The servants of God will mourn. I could speak but am not free to speak to those prejudices that keep us from mourning for public abominations. But they may be easily suggested unto all your thoughts and particularly what they are that have kept us from attending more unto this duty of mourning for public abominations. And give me leave to say that according to the Scripture rule, there is no one of us can have any evidence that we shall escape outward judgments that God will bring for these abominations, if we have not been mourners for them. But that as smart a revenge, as to outward dispensations, may fall upon us as upon those that are most guilty of them, no scripture evidence have we to the contrary. How God may deal with us, I know not.

This then is one part of the duty of this day—that we should humble our souls for all the abominations that are committed in the land of our nativity and, in particular, that we have no more mourned under them.

Our second duty, in reference to this perilous season, is to take care that we be not infected with the evils and sins of it. A man would think it were quite contrary. But really, to the best of my observation, this is and hath been the frame of things, unless upon some extraordinary dispensation of God's spirit: as some men's sins grow very high, other men's graces grow very low. Our Savior hath told us in Matthew 24:12, "Because iniquity shall abound, the love of many shall wax cold." A man would think the abounding of iniquity in the world should give great provocation to love one another. "No," saith our Savior, "the contrary will be found true: as some men's sins grow high, other men's graces will grow low."

And there are these reasons for it:

In such a season, we are apt to have light thoughts of great sins. The prophet looked upon it as a dreadful thing, that upon Jehoiakin's throwing the roll of Jeremiah's prophecy into the fire till it was consumed, yet they were not afraid nor rent their garments, neither the king nor any of his servants that heard all these words (Jeremiah 36:24). They were grown senseless, both of sin and judgment. And where men (be they in other respects ever so wise) can grow senseless of sin, they will quickly grow senseless of judgment too. And I am afraid the great reason why many of us have no impression upon our spirits of danger and perils in the days wherein we live is because we are not sensible of sin.

Men are apt to countenance themselves in lesser evils, having their eyes fixed upon greater abominations of other men that they behold every day; there are those who pay their tribute to the devil—walk in such and such abominations and so countenance themselves in lesser evils. This is part of the public infection that they "do not run out into the same excess of riot that others do," though they live in the omission of duty, conformity to the world, and in many foolish, hurtful, and noisome lusts. They countenance themselves with this that others are guilty of greater abominations.

Pray let such remember this, who have occasion for it (you may know it better than I, but yet I know it by rule, as much as you do by practice) that general converse in the world, in such a season, is full of danger and peril. Most professors are grown of the color and complexion of those with whom they converse.

This is the first thing that makes a season perilous. I know not whether these things may be of concern and use unto you; they seem so to me, and I cannot but acquaint you with them.

II. A second perilous season that we shall hardly come off in is when men are prone to forsake the truth and seducers abound to gather them up that are so, and you will have always these things go together. Do you see seducers abound? You may be sure there is a proneness in the minds of men to forsake the truth, and when there is such a proneness, they will never want seducers—those that will lead off the minds of men from the truth. For there is both the hand of God and Satan in this business. God judicially leaves men when He sees them grow weary of the truth and prone to leave it. And Satan strikes in with the occasion and stirs up seducers. This makes a season perilous. The apostle describes it in 1 Timothy 4:1, "Now the Spirit speaketh expressly, that in the latter times" (these perilous days) "some shall depart from the faith, giving heed to seducing spirits, and doctrines of devils." And so Peter warns them to whom he writes in II Peter 2:1–2 that "there shall come false teachers among them, who privily shall bring in damnable heresies, even denying the Lord that bought them, and bring upon themselves swift destruction; and many shall follow their pernicious ways." There shall come times full of peril, which shall draw men from the truth into destruction.

If it be asked, how may we know whether there be a proneness in the minds of men in any season to depart from the truth? There are three ways whereby we may judge it:

I. The first is that mentioned, 11 Timothy 4:3: "The time will come when they will not endure sound doctrine; but after their own lusts shall they heap to themselves teachers, having itching ears." When men grow weary of sound doctrine—when it is too plain, too heavy, too dull, too common, too high, too mysterious, one thing or other that displeases them, and they would hear something new, something that may please, it is a sign that there are in such an age many who are prone to forsake sound doctrine. And many such we know.

When men have lost the power of truth in their conversation and are as prone and ready to part with the profession of it in their minds. Do you see a man retaining the profession of the truth under a worldly conversation? He wants but refrains from temptation or a seducer to take away his faith from him. An inclination to hearken after novelties and loss of the power of truth in the conversation is a sign of proneness unto this declension from the truth. Such a season, you see, is perilous. And why is it perilous? Because the souls of many are destroyed in it. The apostle tells us directly in II Peter 2:1 of "false prophets among the people, who privily bring in damnable heresies, even denying the Lord that bought them, and bring upon themselves swift destructions." Will it abide there? No. "And many shall follow their pernicious ways, by reason of whom the way of truth shall be evil spoken of."

Brethren, while it is well with us, through the grace of God, and our own houses are not in flames, pray do not let us think the times are not perilous, when so many turn into pernicious errors and fall into swift destruction. Will you say the time of the public plague was not perilous because you were alive? No. Was the fire not dreadful because your houses were not burned? No, you will, notwithstanding, say it was a dreadful plague and a dreadful fire. And pray consider, is not this a perilous season when multitudes have an inclination to depart from the truth and God, in just judgment, hath permitted Satan to stir up seducers to draw them into pernicious ways and their poor souls perish forever?

Besides, there is a great aptness in such a season to work indifference in the minds of those who do not intend utterly to forsake the truth. Little did I think I should ever have lived in this world to find the minds of professors grown altogether indifferent as to the doctrines of God's eternal election, the sovereign efficacy of grace in the conversion of sinners, justification by the imputation of the righteousness of Christ. But many are, as to all these things, grown to an indifference. They know not whether they are so or not. I bless God I know something of the former generation, when professors would not hear of these things without the highest detestation. And now high professors begin to be leaders in it. And it is too much among the best of us. We are not so much concerned for the truth as our forefathers. I wish one could say we were as holy.

This proneness to depart from the truth is a perilous season because it is the greatest evidence of the withdrawing of the Spirit of God from His church. For the Spirit of God is promised to this end "to lead us into all truth." And when the efficacy of truth begins to decay, it is the greatest evidence of the departing and withdrawing of the Spirit of God. And I think that this is a dangerous thing; for if the Spirit of God departs, then our glory and our life depart.

What now is our duty in reference to this perilous season? Forewarnings of perils are given us to instruct us in our duty.

The first is not to be content with what you judge a sincere profession of truth but to labor to be found in the exercise of all those graces that peculiarly respect the truth. There are graces that peculiarly respect the truth that we are to exercise. And if these are not found in our hearts, all our profession will issue in nothing.

And these are:

Love: "Because they loved not the truth." They made profession of the Gospel. But they received not the truth in the love of it. There was want of love of the truth. Truth will do no man good where there is not the love of it. "Speaking the truth in love" is the substance of our Christian profession. Pray, brethren, let us labor to love the truth and to take off all prejudices from our minds, that we may do so.

It is the great and only rule to preserve us in perilous times to labor to have the experience of the power of every truth in our hearts. If so be ye have learned the Lord Jesus. How? So as to "put off the old man, which is corrupt according to the deceitful lusts" and to "put on the new man, which after God is created in righteousness and true holiness," Ephesians 4:22–24. This is to learn the truth. The great grace that is to be exercised with reference to truth in such a season as this is to exemplify it in our hearts in the power of it. Labor for the experience of the power of every truth in your own hearts and lives.

II. Zeal for the truth. Truth is the most proper object for zeal. We ought to "contend earnestly for the truth once delivered to the saints" to be willing, as God shall help us to part with name and reputation and to undergo scorn and contempt all that this world can cast upon us, in giving testimony unto the truth. Everything that this world counts dear and valuable is to be forsaken, rather than the truth. This was the great end for which Christ came into the world.

Cleave unto the means that God hath appointed and ordained for your preservation in the truth. I see some are ready to go to sleep and think themselves not concerned in these things: the Lord awaken their hearts. Keep to the means of preservation in the truth—the present ministry. Bless God for the remainder of a ministry valuing the truth, knowing the truth, sound in the faith—cleave unto them. There is little influence upon the minds of men from this ordinance and institution of God, in the great business of the ministry. But know there is something more in it than that they seem to have better abilities to dispute than you: more knowledge, more light, better understandings than you. If you know no more in the ministry than this, you will never have benefit by it. They are God's ordinance; the name of God is upon them. God will be sanctified in them. They are God's ordinance for the preservation of the truth.

Let us carefully remember the faith of them who went before us in the profession of the last age. I am apt to think there was not a more glorious profession for a thousand years upon the face of the earth than was among the professors of the last age. And pray, what faith were they of? Were they half-Armenian and half-Socinian; half-papist and half I-know-not-what? Remember how zealous they were for the truth. How little their holy souls would have borne with those public defections from the doctrine of truth that we see and do not mourn over but make nothing of in the days wherein we live. God was with them. And they lived to His glory and died in peace: "whose faith follow" and example pursue. And remember the faith they lived and died in: look round about and see whether any of the new creeds have produced a new holiness to exceed theirs.

III. A third thing that makes a perilous season is professors mixing themselves with the world and learning their manners. And if the other perilous seasons are come upon us, this is come upon us also. This was the foundation and spring of the first perilous season that was in the world that first brought in a deluge of sin and then a deluge of misery. It was the beginning of the first public apostasy of the church, which issued in the severest mark of God's displeasure. Genesis 6:2: "The sons of God saw the daughters of men that they were fair; and they took them wives of all which they chose." This is but one instance of the church of God, the sons of God, professors, mixing themselves with the world. This was not all that they took to themselves wives. But this was an instance the Holy Ghost gives that the church in those days did degenerate and mix itself with the world. What is the end of mixing themselves in this manner with the world? Psalms 106:35: "They mingled themselves with the nations." And what then "and learned their manners." If anything under heaven will make a season perilous, this will do it—when we mingle with the world and learn their manners.

# CHAPTER 14

# THE SCOURGE POST

## "Physical Suffering"

The Account Related BY Josephus the Scholar.

Scourging was a horrible thing. Forty lashes were given by both the Jews and the Romans. The Jews always stopped one short of forty because they didn't want to break the law (2 Corinthians 11:24; cf. Deuteronomy 25:3). The Romans gave thirteen lashes across the chest and then thirteen on each shoulder. It usually took two men to do it because one wasn't strong enough to continue the whipping at the desired pace. The victim's hands were tied to a post, so the body slumped. When the scourging was complete, the organs would be exposed. The bleeding was often so profuse that many would die. Jesus suffered a tremendous amount of physical pain before He ever reached the cross.

And so it is related by Josephus, the Jew, who lived shortly after our Lord, that Jesus was torn in His scourging to such a degree that the bones of His ribs were laid bare. It was also revealed by the most Holy Virgin to St. Bridget, in these words: "I, who was standing by, saw His body scourged to the very ribs, so that His ribs themselves might be seen. And what was even yet more bitter still, when the scourges were drawn back, His flesh was furrowed by them." To St. Teresa, Jesus wished to have Him painted exactly as she had seen Him and told the painter to represent a large piece of flesh torn off and hanging down from the left elbow. But when the painter inquired as to the shape in which he ought to paint it, he found, on turning round again to his picture, the piece of flesh already drawn.

Ah, my beloved and adored Jesus, how much hast Thou suffered for love of me. Oh, let not so many pangs and so much blood be lost for me.

## "The Scourging"

"During the second mystery, I cried out, and the dialogue went something like this: 'No! No! Stop that!' For there was our beloved Jesus being pulled to and fro as His tormentors pulled

His upper garment from His back. They tied His wrists together and drove a spike into an upright beam. Jesus's hands were bound by strips of a brown leather like cord. Then the central part of the cord that bound His hands was looped over the spike in the beam. Poor Jesus was pinned by His hands.

"There were five people in this cave like room that appeared to be dug out of a hillside, a sort of hole-room in the hillside.

"I screamed and winced as two soldiers took turns hitting Jesus's bare back with a long brown leatherlike strap. On this strap were metal hooks, laid horizontally all along the strap. These nail-like, clawlike fixtures on the strap cut and scratched deeply into Jesus's flesh, causing blood to pour out. It was a despicable game with the soldiers. They laughed and joked. Jesus never said a word.

"I cried, 'Say something! Say something!' He could save Himself, but Jesus remained silent as they spat and insulted Him. His back became a mass of welts and torn flesh. Jesus was barefoot; His sandals had fallen off as they banged a stake higher into the pole and raised poor Jesus up so His toes barely touched the floor. The floor was just dirt and blood. The soldier remarked, 'Maybe they cut out His lying tongue. Ha, ha!' Our poor Jesus remained silent."

## "A Savior"

The definition of Savior: a person who saves, rescues, or delivers: the savior of the country.

The book of thesaurus says: Jesus, Jesus of Nazareth, the Nazarene, Jesus Christ, Christ, Savior, Saviour, Good Shepherd, Redeemer, Deliverer, Son, Word, Logos, Jew, Hebrew, Israelite, Prophet

Usage: a teacher and prophet born in Bethlehem and active in Nazareth; his life and sermons form the basis for Christianity

## "Could You Die Like Christ?"

I went to a restaurant in the midday with some minister friends of mine. And while we were waiting in line to be served, the Holy Spirit came over me that hit me from the crown of my head to the soles of my feet.

We set down and prepared to order our food, just like we do every month that we would meet. I said something that shocked these men of God. "Could you die like Christ did"? They both looked at me, and I am at them, and there was a bewilderment on their face. The first man said, "I couldn't put nails in my wrist. It would take a lot for that to happen to me, and if someone asked me, I would say no." The next man said the same as the first preacher. Can you ask yourself if you can give up everything for your people and be the Savior of the world? If the answer was no, then you are in good company. That is the right answer.

## "I Am Not Worthy, Are You?"

The Passion of the Christ is a depiction of the life and death of our Savior Jesus Christ. When I went to go see the movie, I was moved with compassion. I could not look upon what Christ had to go through because I felt that I was not worthy. Every stripe that he took were my sins that were poured out of his skin, by his blood. He paid a price he did not owe. I owe a price I will never be able to pay. As the scourging post was spinning him around, I could sense the fibers of his mortal being torn apart, and he would look teary eyed and not saying a word, as every splatter of blood was being spilled onto the floor. When his mother came in to cleanse the temple of his blood, the tears fell as my eyes became swollen. I rushed out of the theatre in agony and pain as I fell to the ground.

Was I asking for God to forgive me and to rededicate my life to him and to take up my cross and follow him? I perceive the answer was yes to the question. Just like the question that was posed to those two ministers about dying like Christ did. Over two weeks later on, the call in my life meant to deal with the dire consequences of his death. I went back in, but I told my spouse at that time that I am sorry and for what I have done forgive me as she later on found out that I was a deceiver to myself and my family. Sometimes the spilling of blood will open up the eyes of a lost soul. We look at life sometimes as we see our lives swaying on the side of God, but our deeds tell the opposite, I am afraid. When your compassion is on the one who died for you and I.

This took place in Bethany beyond the Jordan, where John was baptizing. The next day, he saw Jesus coming toward him and said, "Behold, the Lamb of God, who takes away the sin of the world!" (John 1:28–29).

"This is my commandment: love one another as I love you. No one has greater love than this, to lay down his life for his friends" (John 15:12–13).

Jesus Christ, the eternal Son of God, entered time and history through the Incarnation. "The Word became flesh and dwelt among us, full of grace and truth" (John 1:14). Jesus Christ, the Son of God (Mark 1:1; Romans 1:4), is a gift of love from the Father for the salvation of the world (John 3:16–17), the one who died for all of mankind (2 Corinthians). Jesus Christ, the Lamb of God, fulfills the Old Testament prophecy. The Lamb of God recalls the Passover lamb, whose blood was sprinkled on the houses of the Israelites to protect them during the Exodus from Egypt (Exodus 12). The Messiah as the suffering servant will give his life as an offering for sin (Isaiah 53). The lamb anticipates the victorious lamb of the Apocalypse (Revelation 5–7; 5:15), our "Savior, the Lord Jesus Christ" (Philippians 3:21).

The paschal mystery in the Gospel of John reveals Christ as the new Adam. "One of the soldiers thrust a lance into his side and immediately blood and water came out" (John19:34). Eve came from the side of the first Adam. The open side of the new Adam is the beginning of the new definitive community of men with one another, a New Covenant in Christ, symbolized by water and blood, the sacraments of baptism and the lamb's supper,

"I am the Bread of Life. He who comes to me shall not hunger, and he who believes in me shall never thirst" (John 6:35).

# CHAPTER 15

# THE CRUCIFIXION

Although the Romans did not invent crucifixion, they perfected it as a form of torture and capital punishment that was designed to produce a slow death with maximum pain and suffering. It was one of the most disgraceful and cruel methods of execution and usually was reserved only for slaves, foreigners, revolutionaries, and the vilest of criminals. Roman law usually protected Roman citizens from crucifixion, except perhaps in the case of desertion by soldiers.

(The cross) was characterized by an upright post and a horizontal crossbar, and it had several variations. It was customary for the condemned man to carry his own cross from the flogging post to the site of crucifixion outside the city walls. He was usually nakcd, unless this was prohibited by local customs. Since the weight of the entire cross was probably well over 300 lb. (136 kg), only the crossbar was carried.

## "The Crossbar"

Was God trying to give us a correlation from the time of Abraham his only begotten son, when they climbed Mt. Moriah, the following items were on Issacs' back? There was a crossbar that went across his back, shoulder to shoulder, there were thorns and thistles used to keep the fire going for the sacrifice. Abraham carried a knife in a sheath and a flint to ignite the fire. They both went up the hill and were looking for something to sacrifice. In most cases it was a red heifer or a ram without spot or blemish. When they get to the top of the mountain and would perform (in Hebrew tongue) Shentavta – the mercy killing. In order to sacrifice a lamb or ram you would cut the throat from ear to ear. Abraham would then drain out all the blood. He would then sprinkle the blood on the alter to God. Isn't it strange that Mt. Mariah was the opposite place of Golgotha where they found Adams' skull? This is also the place where Jesus Christ would be crucified. If I was telling the story and putting in dialogue, this is how the dialogue would go.

As a 12-year-old boy and his father were trudging up the hill with a crossbeam on his back and the thorns and thistles were attached to the beam. This 12-year-old boy would say to his father, Father how long before we reach the top? The father said, not very long son, not very long. As they finally reach the peak of the Mountain known as Mariah, Isaac looks around.

He says to his father where is the ram or the heifer? As his father instructs Isaac to remove everything, lay the cross beam on the ground and put the thorns and thistles on the grill. He then uses his knife and flint to start a fire with the thorns and thistles. Then he instructs his son to take the crossbeam and lay it on the ground opposite the fire. As he lays his son across the crossbeam, Isaac says to him, father why are you doing this? Abraham intends to cut Issacs' throat from ear to ear with his knife. He hears a sound from Heaven like a mighty wind that says, Abraham do not lay hold onto thy son. For I see that you are willing to sacrifice your only begotten son and I will provide for you this day the sacrifice that is needed. There was a red heifer caught in the thorns and thistles and the crown of his head was covered with blood. His feet and hooves were also covered in blood. As Abraham takes Isaac off the crossbeam, he placed the red heifer onto the crossbeam and performed the mercy killing. Abraham says to Isaac as he holds him fast, I told you God would provide.

Can you see that God also is going to do the same thing by providing his only begotten son in place of the red heifer?

## "The Via Della Rosa"

Earlier I showed you how Romans crucified people. Hollywood and the heathens and Jews would want you to believe that Jesus went down the Via Della Rosa with a 300-pound cross. Here is a man who weighed about 158 pounds according to science. He was 5'8 or 5'9" and was just beaten and every part of his body was open. He had over 6 trials that he had to go to. The stress level had to be amazing. Even in the garden of Gethsemane, which is called the place of the olive press, Jesus sweat platelets of blood. Because of his weakened condition even the angels had to minister to him to allow him to take this cup of suffering. Before the second trial began he was beaten by the Jewish guards. His beard was torn off his face by their powerful hands, his face was beaten so bad that his body contorted, and his eyes were swollen shut and this face was unrecognizable.

Getting back to the cross, how can this scientifically make sense? I go along with what the Romans did to a condemned person. I believe that the time that Jesus was scourged that he was naked before mankind. I believe that they did give him a crossbeam which went from shoulder to shoulder for him to carry the weight of the 75-pound beam. He was forced to carry it up the hill called the place of the scull – Golgotha. Along the Via Della Rosa because of his weakening condition this prophet/teacher fell. Trying to regain his composure he fell again. Then for the final third time he fell and could not get up. They were not allowed to beat him because he had already received the maximum at the scourging post. There was a man there for the Passover whose is named Simon and was a Samaritan Jew. The dialogue would have gone something like this with Jesus. As the guard yelled for the man to pick up the crossbar off Jesus. But sir, I do not know this man said Simon. Would you rather be crucified in his place the guard said? Simon immediately took the crossbeam from Jesus shoulders and Jesus reached behind him to hold himself up and says to Simon with a soft gurgully voice, Simon, take up my cross and walk with me. Simon began to cry as he carried his cross down the Via Della Rosa – The Road of Suffering.

As Jesus and Simon and the guards are all on the hillside the captain of the guards rides up on his mount and says to the other guard, why haven't you brought the long pole for the cross? The guard said my lord, the Jews told us that they could not make this cross for this man because it was the Passover. As he turns towards the trees and points towards the tree he commands – cut this tree down and strip it bare. We do not have time to finish this cross off, so we will nail this crossbeam to this tree. The guard said to him, but my Lord, all the splinters will go into his back. The captain said my name is Cornelius and I am the captain of the guards and my job is to make sure that it is a successful execution. Then Jesus rose up and in his mind, he cursed the tree and quoted out of Deuteronomy, curseth is a man that hangeth from a tree. The name of the tree that Jesus cursed was a dogwood tree. And to present date they do not grow over 6 – 8 feet tall. Then he lowered his head. So as the guards took the crossbeam and nailed it to the tree on the ground, they took Jesus and laid him on the cross. They made sure that the seat that is usually there was in fact there to help sustain his weight on the cross.

As I told you earlier in the story, the Romans were very good at what they did, and they were very sadistic.

## "The Hollow Cavity"

Hollywood, the Jews and the Heathens would want you to think that when they nailed Jesus to the cross that they put the nails in his hands. That is not true. For he would have fallen off the cross because there are not enough bones in the hand to support the weight of a man if attached at the hand. Doctors have proven beyond a shadow of a doubt through their studies and research that even in present day and time, that the only way to support a body on the cross was by putting the nails through the wrist.

They call that the narrow or hollow cavity that will not only allow the support on the cross but also to make death very fast. With bursting of arteries and veins, anyone would slowly die of not only loss of blood, but scientists have proven they have used rusty nails and the person could get tetanus from the rusty nails. Before the nails were put into his hands what was Jesus thinking? After all, did he not come down here to set everything right that was wrong by the evil one? Jesus looked up and saw Satan with a hammer in his hand and behind him was a row and string of people with hammers in their hands. As he saw Eve then Adam and then Cain, then Abraham and Isaac and Jacob and the 12 tribes and all the kings and that was on the right side of the cross. Then he turned to the left and he saw people like: Genghis Khan, Hitler, George Souris, all the Bush's, homosexuals, prostitutes, drug addicts, murders, adulterers, coveters, truce breakers who all had hammers in their hands. Then at his feet were people with the mark of the beast who also had hammers in their hands along with the Antichrist and Satan. Then he smiled. As he could feel the pain of everyone of these people, one by one until he was nailed to the cross. A horn was sounded to announce to the governor that the third person was being crucified. The cross was then raised with ropes by three guards until it landed in the hole to make it secure. In the 12th hour, again the mystery of the number 12 shows up, Jesus was placed between 2 men. Cries were heard from the patrons all around and tears were shed at this blasphemer, Jesus. The guard got onto a ladder as the guards below were casting lots for Jesus garments but Cornelius the captain of the guards kept his purple robe, like his future depended on it. The guard placed a plaque above Jesus head which read, King of the Jews in Hebrew, Greek and Latin. And the dialogue would have gone this way. As the people and the pharisees raised their fists in anger and one of the pharisees closest to Mary said, he is not our king. We have only one King and his name is Caesar. The crowd jeered on and Cornelius motioned to the guards to control the crowd. Cornelius said if I hear any more uproar I'm going to put 10 crosses up here. Silence loomed from the crowd immediately.

**"Jesus Speaks From the Cross"**

Jesus looked down at his mother and said with a gasping voice, mother this is your son as he turned his head towards John. Jesus said to John this is your mother, take her away. Have her remember me the way I was not the way I am. They departed hence there away from the crowd. Then the pharisee close to Mary said, if you be the messiah then come down. As Jesus was looking around in his own mind he said, I endured everything father for you, even to the point of the cross. I have defeated man instead of man defeating me. Then Jesus thought, who are the people he had made a difference in their lives.

**"Jesus Reminiscing"**

As Jesus was on the cross he could hear the sounds from the other two men on the crosses from the attack of the insects and the birds that were pecking at their eyes. For they too were naked on the cross for their insurrection against the state of Rome. As the third hour is approaching (on the cross) Jesus begins to remember all the things he had accomplished for his father. There was remorse in his face. He began to see the 100,000's and 100,000's of Jewish Christians who had been slaughtered by the Romans for believing in him. He would see Peter one day being crucified upside down. Then he would see

Solomon's Temple of 70 AD be destroyed so that not one stone was not left upon another. He would see the abomination of desolation that was spoken about by the prophet Daniel.

## "Future Tense"

As the tears began to trickle down Jesus cheek he could see into the future of those who would die for his name sake. He saw 50,000,000 Christians die during the time of the dark ages from the Catholic church. The burning of christians at Salem. The black people that were beaten, persecuted and murdered for the color of their skin. The Jewish people, by the Nazis as he saw rows and rows of people looking through a fence with sunken eye sockets, in the back ground a picture of them burning the bodies. Then Jesus began to cry out louder as he saw something that is so frightful, the 72,000,000 babies aborted. Lastly those that would die for his namesake by being beheaded. Then Jesus looked to the right at the man on the cross and the man spoke to him. He said to Jesus, Jesus you are a righteous man. We deserve what we have gotten as he raised himself up on the seat to take a breath. You did nothing. Then a voice from the other cross said he deserves everything because he broke the law of Moses. The man spoke to Jesus and said Jesus will you remember me when we enter paradise? Jesus with all his faculties said to the man, so shall I remember you when I enter paradise along with you.

## "The Proof of the Crucifixion"

In the beginning of the chapter we talked about the Romans and how they crucified condemned criminals. One of the things that I told you was that they would always make sure it was a successful crucifixion beyond a shadow of a doubt. They would take the body and make sure it was in a Y position dangling down from the cross. This way your arms would get to the point that your shoulders would be dislocated. They made sure their knees were protruding outward to only be able to catch a breath by lifting their body up to the seat and resting their body. So how do we really know that Christ died on the cross? Even up to today people have believed that the crucifixion and the resurrection never happened. Even renowned scientists had begun modern day studies on the crucifixion. They were Atheist and Agnostic. One thing they did do was, they concluded that when someone died on the cross, it was a successful execution. There are theologists that date back to the time of Martin Luther who have said that there are 9,000 prophecies on just one man come true.

## "Jesus Gives up the Ghost"

As Jesus began to cry out to his father, my God, my God, why has thou forsaken me? As Jesus looks at his left shoulder and sees the sins of the world and then to his right shoulder and the same for the past, present and future. As the angel of death is coming for Jesus the skies begin to grow dark and ominous and there was lightning, and thunder mixed with rain. As the angel of death hovers over Jesus and places his hand over his head, then Jesus looks up to Heaven and says with his last bated breath, Father into thy hand I commit my spirit. It is finished. As the ground begins to shake uncontrollably and Cornelius is knocked off his horse, off in the distance you can see Solomon's temple being destroyed but not all the way. In the Holies of Holies, the 14-inch curtain was rent and raved from top to bottom. At that moment Jesus' head and his body grew limp, as his body began to release all the bodily fluids as an indication of death.

## "The Myth of Good Friday"

A lot of theologists, scholars, teachers of religion would make you think that Jesus died on Friday. That assumption is not true. For if that was true, and Jesus said, as Jonah was in the belly of the whale for 3 days and 3 nights so shall the son of man be in the earth for 3 days and 3 nights. So, let's look at this from a scientific standpoint. Jesus died at the 3rd hour or 3:00 of the day. So, if he died on Friday at 3:00 we would then count Saturday, Sunday and Monday. So that means that he wasn't resurrected on Sunday, so that wouldn't work. Here is what really did happen. The Passover was Tuesday when they had the Seder meal. Wednesday morning Jesus was arrested. By Wednesday at noon he was already on the cross. At 3:00 that afternoon Jesus was dead, according to all that is scientific data. So, let's check our theory out. Jesus died on Wednesday at 3:00. Thursday, Friday and on Saturday at 3:00 he arose from the dead. While in the tomb the angels and the heavenly host were preparing Jesus to arise as El Elyon or the immortal high priest by the order of Melchizedek of Salem. That would make more sense, don't you think? So, since no one could buy or sell on the High Sabbath from Friday sundown to Saturday sundown, they had to wait until after to buy the materials that would be necessary for the embalming of Jesus Christ.

## "Scientific Proof Jesus is Dead"

Because it was the time of the Passover and the governor didn't want those people hanging on the cross for people to see, he commissioned the captain of the guard to have the guards break the legs of the 2 thieves', so they couldn't rise and catch a breath. They would eventually within minutes suffocate in their own blood. Then the took the cross and laid it down, pulled the nails out postmortem and throw their bodies into a pit to be eaten by the birds and wild animals. When they went to the cross of Christ to break his legs he was already dead which fulfilled the prophecy found in Psalms 22. This said, when they came to break the legs of Christ, he was already dead so not one bone was broken. For all you naysayers out there that don't believe in the crucifixion and the resurrection, at the Mayo Clinic in Minnesota there were some top-notch scientists from MIT as well as Harvard graduates. They have not only done studies on afterlife successfully, but also on the crucifixion and its' aftermath. Here is what they said. They said upon death you have 11 major organs and your blood begins to try to save the organs by creating a peridium sack. Cornelius asked one of his guards with a 5-foot spear to make sure it was a successful execution. They could reach up and thrust the spear through his side, up his ribs and into his heart. By that time the water that was mixed with blood began to trickle out as the sack broke and gushed out all over a soldier. That was the indication that the guard nodded to Cornelius that Jesus was dead. Before they began to lower his body and take out the nails post mortem, Joseph of Arimathea said to Cornelius, I have and edict from the governor to remove this body of Jesus into my tomb as he handed the order to Cornelius. We will take over from here. As Joseph and his household with ropes and hammers removed the nails, his crown of thorns on his head, and wrapped his naked body in a shroud to be placed in a tomb.

## "Footnotes"

Well as you see everything that the Romans said they were going to do they accomplished. And Jesus is dead. So all of you naysayers, atheists, agnostics that don't believe that he was crucified and died, I have some swampland I would like to sell to you. So many stories from Hollywood, the Vatican, Theologists have been distorted. Why? This storyteller doesn't really know but it was distorted. To recap everything, we have given you a blow by blow description from the beginning of being accused to Jesus' death. My question to you is – is it fact or fiction?

# CHAPTER 16

# GEHENNA

**"Jesus Gives up the Ghost and Heads for Gehenna"**

Before we start with this chapter I want to clarify what the definition of Gehenna means: all I have always tried to do throughout this book is to be truthful and honest with you. Everybody believes that God created Hell. It is found in the deep recesses of the core of the earth. But that is not true. After Satan fell, God created a place of confinement, for the fallen angels and Satan. If you go and commit a crime do you go directly to prison and then get judged? Or do they confine you in a place that you can't escape from until you go to trial? I believe that it is the latter of the two. I believe that there have been many Christians of modern day that have gone to Hell or Gehenna as they said it was. They saw jail cells. The dark void of emptiness which to me is a separation from God. I believe that Hell has not been made yet. But that is another book.

So as Jesus' ghost was led by the angel of death to this dark, dreary place you could see him going through all the fires and he could see the separation between Gehenna and paradise. He noticed because God created Gehenna that his journey would find him in the place called the Leg of Gehenna. Just like Jesus has a body, so did Satan. As the angel of death at his side followed him down, Jesus' ghost then stood on the leg and deposited all the sins that were ever created by mankind for the past, the present and the future. Jesus did something that was very unusual but did fulfill the scriptures. The first scripture that he fulfilled was found in the book of Psalms 88. He took all the sins to the lowest part of the earth or Gehenna. But then he did something that only God could do. As he rolled around, and all the sins of the world were thrown as far as to the East and to the West and neither shall twain. Psalms 103:12.

### "Jesus Opens up Paradise"

Josephus was one of the scholars back at the time of Jesus Christ. If anyone could substantiate that Jesus Christ was born, died, went to Gehenna and opened paradise it would have been Josephus that is found in the works of Josephus. In the works of Josephus, he stated that for months all around Jerusalem that the people like Moses, Abraham, Isaac and the patriarchs were seen walking around Jerusalem and even spoke with people. As a matter of fact, it even says that the number of people they saw were up to about 500. So now we have a truthful document that can back up this marvelous claim. There are so many people in this world even today that don't believe that this could happen. But it did happen.

Meanwhile the Ghost of Jesus and the Angel of Death appear at the Gates of Paradise. Jesus looks over to a place called Shoel and sees Gehenna in operation. As the tears trickle down his cheek, even as a ghost and he sees all the people that are trapped in this bottomless abyss. The dialogue would go something like this. From the group of condemned souls as they yell, Jesus take us from this place. We have learned our lesson. Then through the earths' core arrives Satan. He holds on to the keys around his belt of death and hell. Jesus says, Satan you wicked and slothful servant. Where is your sting now Satan? For I have defeated you. Not only in life but also in death. As the angel of death extends his hand towards Satan and the keys of death and hell have now miraculously shown up in Jesus' hands. And then with one swift movement he says to Satan, leave this land and go back to the atmosphere. This is where you have been sent and not where you are now. You do have a time when you will be trapped down here but that time is not now. As Satan tries to get his last word in, Jesus shuts his mouth and with a flick of the wrist he is gone. Then you could hear the cheers of all those who went to paradise from the time of Adam to the last person on the cross. Then Jesus opens the gates and looses them from their prison. Meanwhile on earth people are preparing for the burial of Jesus when they see all those that died roaming the streets.

# CHAPTER 17

# THE RISE OF EL ELYON

Meanwhile Jesus is being prepared to be El Elyon, the high priest of the immortal God. Jesus says to his angels, tomorrow will be the third day, so we have a lot to do. Michael, he says, is everything ready on Mt. Zion? Michael says to Jesus, El Elyon everything is ready and prepared for you. The angels are excited that you are coming home, and I am too. For I miss my Father and the Holy Spirit. Then they all broke bread with Jesus and a cup of nectar. After they discarded the table, the throne and any of the utensils that were left, they began the ceremony. The first thing they did was put the miter hat on his head. Then they put the bind around his neck as they attached the fob with the 12 stones. Then they put a form of a tallit over his head and then put on the robe. They buttoned each button until it would reach the floor. The angels began to leave one by one except for Raphael and Gabriel, then Jesus said to Gabriel we have to do something different to show woman's strength. Remember when I helped Deborah rule over a nation of stiff necked men of Israel and Gabriel said yes. Jesus said you know these blind guides and the white washed sepulchers, they have love on the outside but dried up old men bones on the inside. They tried to bring false witness against me. I will do something that they will never accept, having any women as witnesses. So, when I come out of the tomb tomorrow which will be at 3:00, the same time I died, they will be coming from the temple and will begin to prepare my body for burial. You will tell them that I have risen, and those two witnesses will be my witnesses to the apostles and to the world of my resurrection.

## "Two Witnesses"

At the end of the high Sabbath, about 6:30 PM you would be able to now buy or sell goods according to the law of Moses. Mary of Bethany and Mary of the town of Magdalene were approaching the tomb and noticed that the Roman and Jewish guards were running away towards Jerusalem. When they approached the tomb of Joseph of Arimathea, this is what the dialogue would probably sound like. As a young woman arrayed in purple garments entered the tomb first and said Mary, the tomb has been broken open. They both noticed that the seal was broken. They both entered the tomb and they heard a sound of angels and on the cold slab were two angels. The first angel – Gabriel blew his horn as they were both in fright. Gabriel said to the two women, why do you look for the living among the dead? For El Elyon is how we know him, but you know him as Jesus on earth, he has risen as he told you he would. Go tell his disciples the same thing. Be witness to the four corners of the earth. Tell them that he will come again. Mary of Magdalene drops her basket of supplies for burial and she hurries off to tell the apostles that he has risen. Mary of Bethany with dark black hair and a green robe went into the tomb and asked Gabriel, can I see his shroud that he laid on the cold slab? Gabriel says yes and hands the shroud to her. Then as the fiery cherubim known as Raphael tells Mary, you will be his witness as the last high priest. He points up the hill and says go, he is waiting for you.

What is interesting about the two women as witnesses is theoretically according to Jewish law, it is impossible for a woman to be a witness for anything. In the story earlier when Jesus was accused by two men falsely for the crimes against the Jewish nation, then why could it not be possible for Jesus to do the opposite? So, Mary departed and began to head up the hill.

Meanwhile, by now Mary of Magdalene has reached the house where the apostles are cowering. She knocks on the door, she says, please (quietly) Peter, John open the door for I have some good news. As Peter opens the door and allows her to come in, with her out of breath from running, she says He has risen, excitedly. Simon a small meek little man with a receded hairline says to Mary, woman what are you talking about. You know according to the law of Moses that women can never be a witness to anything good or bad. As she begins to hug Peter and looks into his eyes, Peter she says, you know I tell you the truth. The Master has risen. The angels told us as we began to prepare his burial and found him not there. Peter she said (softly) they called him El Elyon, for we know him on this earth as Jesus. As Peter and many of the apostles began to raise their hands to heaven and shouted: Jesus, Jesus, Jesus. They all opened the door and ran frantically towards the tomb.

## "Jesus Begins to Ascend to Heaven"

As Mary of Bethany was walking up the hill she noticed a man in high priest apparel. She extended her hand towards him and said to him, please sir tell us what you have done with our master, so we can prepare his burial and put him back in the tomb. She began to cry, and a voice as it begins to turn towards her says, Mary why do you weep and why do you look for the living among the dead? She remembered the words were the same as the angels had said. She cries out with a loud voice Rabboni which means master in Hebrew as she begins with open arms to hug Jesus. Then he extends his right hand towards Mary as she is running up to greet him. She notices he has a gold chalice under his vesper in his left hand. He then says to Mary, Mary do not touch me for I have not ascended to your father and my father. Then Mary smiles as Jesus tells her, Mary I must take this blood of my own that was sacrificed for remission of sin to heaven at the Holies of Holies on Mt. Zion. Tell my brethren they will see me again and to meet me in the upper room. Then Jesus vanishes out of sight. As the apostles and Mary all enter the tomb and see two angels sitting on the slab as the sounds of the heavenly host was singing in the background, He is Risen,

He is Risen, El Elyon is Risen. Then Gabriel sounded his shofar as a bright light shines down from Heaven onto the apostles. Go to the upper room. Wait. Jesus will return.

### "Jesus in Heaven"

As the high priest El Elyon approaches the gates he can see the symbols of the different stones of each tribe and the cheers can be heard in the background as the gate is opened for him. The angels are shouting El Elyon, El Elyon, El Elyon as the Heavenly Host joined in unison with them. Jesus walks through the gates where there are streets of gold. The angels have their swords above him as he enters the city. The sound is so deafening from the angels and those that were brought out of paradise. Jesus carries the gold chalice almost over his head as he walks through the crowd and finds himself on top of Mt. Zion.

"The Father and the Holy Ghost Join Him"

As El Elyon reaches the top of Mt. Zion the dialogue would go something like this:

Father we did everything that we were going to do, and it is finished. Now receive my fleshly blood. Then as Jesus was preparing to go into the holies of holies he noticed that even his father had holes in his wrists and in his feet. As he peers to the left of the father, so same does the Holy Spirit. His father says to his son, El Elyon, well done my good and faithful servant. As Jesus enters the holies of holies and sprinkles his blood for all the sins of the world, he then comes out of the holies of holies with an empty chalice. As Michael the archangel receives the chalice from him, he then transforms himself with a white robe and golden sandals and the keys of hell and death now hang around his waistband. He hugs his father and then turns to the holy spirit and hugs him as well. Then he looks into the holy spirits eyes and says they are waiting for you my friend. Help them spread the word. Then the Father and the Son looked down from Mt. Zion.

**The End**

**Footnotes:**

A lot of people who will read this book will look at this book with a sense of assurity that almost everything is real, and a lot is a writers' embellishment. Then a lot of you will read it and see a story that did happen, and all the characters are real. The Dead Sea Scrolls revealed it. I have read the Bible so many times in my 38 years of being in the ministry. I realize that only the truth is going to set you free. We live in a world that has lost track of who is in charge. We are desensitized to everything and anything. I wrote this book to open your eyes but most importantly your heart. Is this truth, fact or fiction?

# ABOUT THE AUTHOR

 Reverend Gary Emas has been associated with the Bread of Life Outreach Ministries since 1991. He is now in his late 60's, married to his recent bride and co-author Micki Emas. They currently reside in Bolingbrook, Illinois and operates his ministry.

For the last 27 years Reverend Gary Emas has had not only a prophetic ministry but also a healing ministry. As a Jew for Christ and Levite, he dates his family back to the time of Moses as a Greek Jew. His legacy consists of: his three children, three grandchildren and now his three step children and 5 step grandchildren. My wife Micki is my co-author and editor.

Reverend Gary Emas is not only an author of his own books: Soteria to Sozo: Cradle to the Grave in 2007, The Last High Priest 2016 and his new book El Elyon 2018, soon to become a motion picture. He also carries the attribute of screen writer and play write. He is very soon going to be working on his 4th and 5th book.